THE POWER OF THE HOLY SPIRIT'S NAMES

TONY EVANS

HARVEST HOUSE PUBLISH
EUGENE, OREGON

T0052381

Unless otherwise indicated, all Scripture quotations are taken from the (NASB®) New American Standard Bible®, Copyright © 1960, 1971, 1977, 1995 by The Lockman Foundation. Used by permission. All rights reserved. www.lockman.org.

Scripture quotations marked NIV are taken from the Holy Bible, New International Version®, NIV®. Copyright © 1973, 1978, 1984, 2011 by Biblica, Inc.® Used by permission of Zondervan. All rights reserved worldwide. www.zondervan.com. The "NIV" and "New International Version" are trademarks registered in the United States Patent and Trademark Office by Biblica, Inc.®

Cover design by Faceout Studio, Spencer Fuller

Cover photo © by Sentavio, Sandra_M / Shutterstock

Interior design by KUHN Design Group

For bulk, special sales, or ministry purchases, please call 1-800-547-8979.
Email: Customerservice@hhpbooks.com

This logo is a federally registered trademark of the Hawkins Children's LLC. Harvest House Publishers, Inc., is the exclusive licensee of this trademark.

The Power of the Holy Spirit's Names
Copyright © 2022 by Tony Evans
Published by Harvest House Publishers
Eugene, Oregon 97408
www.harvesthousepublishers.com

ISBN 978-0-7369-7962-7 (pbk.)
ISBN 978-0-7369-7963-4 (eBook)

Library of Congress Control Number: 2022939209

All rights reserved. No part of this publication may be reproduced, stored in a retrieval system, or transmitted in any form or by any means—electronic, mechanical, digital, photocopy, recording, or any other—except for brief quotations in printed reviews, without the prior permission of the publisher.

Printed in the United States of America

23 24 25 26 27 28 29 30 / BP / 10 9 8 7 6 5 4

ACKNOWLEDGMENTS

I want to thank my friends at Harvest House Publishers for their long-standing partnership in bringing my thoughts, study, and words to print. I particularly want to thank Bob Hawkins for his friendship over the years, as well as his pursuit of excellence in leading his company. I also want to publicly thank Kim Moore and Jean Bloom for their help in the editorial process. In addition, my appreciation goes out to Heather Hair for her skills and insights in collaboration on this manuscript.

CONTENTS

INTRODUCTION

The Holy Spirit is the most misunderstood, marginalized, misused, and underappreciated member of the Trinity. On the one hand, He's ignored, and on the other hand, He's illegitimately sensationalized. Both extremes cancel or limit His work in and through God's people. That's why it's important for us to not only know the Holy Spirit more but as He really is.

The Spirit has a central role in the life of the believer and the empowerment of the church, with the distinctive task of making the reality and truth of God experienced in both. And because He possesses emotions, intellect, and will, He is to be related to on a personal level. He's to be *known*, not merely considered a force or power to be manipulated or used. Although He's nonmaterial, intangible, and invisible, He is nonetheless real and relational.

As with the other two members of the Trinity, one of the best means to understand, appreciate, and benefit from the person of the Holy Spirit is to explore the names and attribute descriptions He's given in Scripture. They explain how He lives those roles in us, through us, and for us.

My first goal in this book, then, is to identify, explain, and illustrate the Holy Spirit and His work through those descriptions and names. By the way, while some of the Holy Spirit's names and descriptions are not always capitalized as proper nouns as I write—just as they aren't in Scripture or at least in some Bible translations or paraphrases—they are nevertheless as significant to our study as if they were.

A second goal is to show believers how to relate to the person of the Holy Spirit in a more personal and intimate way. And a third goal is to help us learn how to take full advantage of all the Spirit offers for our physical lives, our emotional lives, and most importantly, our spiritual lives. When we grasp how to do this, His availability can be maximized for our personal and collective growth and impact.

When we come to know the Spirit—again, not only more but as He really is—we can more intimately tap into the unique ways God reveals Himself to us. That's why we all need to understand that to the degree we take the person and work of the Holy Spirit seriously is the degree to which we will experience more of God.

1

THE HELPER

Just two months after my wife of nearly 50 years passed, I was scheduled to film a Bible study in Sedona, Arizona. In the years prior to her becoming ill, Lois and I had enjoyed traveling to various places around the country for me to film these studies. It gave us some much-needed time away in beautiful locations while also allowing me to work. I had come to look forward to these trips because she was with me.

But this journey would be different. This filming would be difficult. This act of faith, on my part, would take everything I had in me to carry out.

I'd counseled enough people over my four decades as a pastor to know I needed to go. I needed to follow the same advice I'd given to so many others over the years. I had to create new experiences that would enable me to heal during this time of grieving rather than get stuck in an emotional loop. But I'd also counseled enough people to know that doing so is never easy. And the full realization of this truth hit me as I walked down the airport corridor to catch my flight that very first time without Lois.

I walked alone. I pulled my luggage alone. My head hung down, and my heart joined it. And as I moved forward, I grew even more discouraged and depressed to the point that tears welled up in my eyes. I didn't want to go without her. I didn't want to "create new experiences" if Lois wasn't going to be in them. Nor did I feel like teaching on the Bible at that moment in time.

But I would soon find out that, even though I walked alone, I wasn't alone. The Holy Spirit was with me. And like the Holy Spirit knows to do, He met me right where I was with just what I needed to keep going.

As I walked slower and slower by the step, a middle-aged couple I'd never seen before approached me. I didn't know them at all but, as I found out later, they listened to me on the radio. And while people often approach me in airports to say hello or to tell me they listen to me on the radio, these two were different. They didn't say any of that at the start. They didn't tell me their story. They didn't ask for a photo. They simply asked if they could pray for me.

"Well," I answered, realizing they must have been sent by God, "sure."

They put their arms around me, and I put my arms around them. The woman began to weep, and the man began to pray. I'll never forget his words: "Lord, we believe You have led us to our brother today to pray for him. We don't believe we passed by here due to chance. Whatever help and comfort he needs, for whatever he's facing in light of what's happened and what he's going through, I pray that Your Spirit will lift him up and give that help and comfort to him right now."

The gentleman closed his prayer, and then the three of us hugged. After thanking them and hearing some of their kind words about listening to me preach over the years and their condolences for my late wife, Lois, I continued on my way filled with a greater strength than I'd had just moments before. I had driven to the airport completely down. I'd entered the airport terminal completely down. But the Holy Spirit knew I needed help, and at the right time and in the right place, He sent the right people to come and lift me up in prayer so I could keep going.

I was able to do the teaching in Sedona as planned. And while it was by far one of the more difficult things I've ever had to do, I found the subject of knowing God encouraging as I taught through it. In this space of great loss, as I remained obedient to Him despite the pain I was feeling, God peeled back the layers of pain and grief enough to help me see His presence in His Spirit like I needed to.

In fact, when I arrived at the hotel where I would be staying, a woman there encouraged me as well. An employee at the hotel, she overheard my name when I was about to check in, then personally greeted me, expressed her condolences, and let me know she would be praying for me too.

GOD SENDS THE HELPER

The Holy Spirit knows what you need and when you need it, especially when you need it—and Him—the most. After all, we all face times when we're down, when we're in what I'll call a slump.

When baseball players run into a slump, they've entered an extended period of time when they're unable to hit the ball well. They show up game after game after game, following the prescribed routine, yet each time at the plate seems to nurture the self-fulfilling prophecy taking root in their minds. They ground out, pop up, or fly out over and over again. Worse, they might strike out. No matter how hard they try, they just can't manage a base hit let alone a home run. Sometimes they're even sent down to the minor leagues until they figure out how to overcome this slump.

Whether routine creates grooves so deep that they drag us into a mental rut or we experience what feels like debilitating pain, slumps happen to all of us. These are the times joy seems to be missing. When deliverance seems distant. When strength seems depleted. Maybe what you hoped would happen hasn't happened, at least not yet. You keep traipsing up to the plate, bat in hand, only to swing at the air, "striking out." You're just not connecting anymore with what matters.

Jesus knew we would all face spiritual slumps. He knew there would be days, weeks, or even years when His people would feel disconnected. He especially knew this would happen to His own band of close disciples when He was crucified and then left their physical presence. That's why He called them aside to meet with them in an upper, secluded room, where He talked about what He planned to do about it. He wanted to give them the tools to thrive even when He was no longer physically by their side.

Jesus also knew His disciples were sad. He could see it on their faces and hear it in their voices. That's why He began His conversation with calming words. "Do not let your heart be troubled," He assured them (John 14:1). He went on to talk about His leaving and to tell them He was going ahead to prepare a place for them.

Then Jesus introduced them to the person and work of the Holy Spirit. He said, "I will ask the Father, and He will give you another Helper, that He may be with you forever; that is the Spirit of truth, whom the world cannot receive, because it does not see Him or know Him, but you know Him because He abides with you and will be in you" (John 14:16-17).

Jesus introduces the Holy Spirit to His disciples through the interesting phrase *another Helper*. We'll fully explore the Spirit's name Helper, but first let's look at the word *another*.

During that period in biblical culture, two common Greek terms were used when referencing another, but Jesus intentionally used the one indicative of a same, like manner—or similar kind. This was to emphasize the reality that even though He was leaving them, God was sending someone exactly like Him to help them through each upcoming day, week, month, and year. In being similar, He, the Holy Spirit, would bear all the attributes of deity Christ had as well.

The disciples weren't fully familiar with the concept of the Trinity at this time, so the introduction of the Holy Spirit probably caught them off guard. As I mentioned in the Introduction to this book, the Holy Spirit is the third person of the Trinity. God is a triune Being. He exists as God the Father, God the Son, and God the Holy Spirit. While existing as one God, He also consists of three co-equal persons who are one in essence while simultaneously distinct in role and personality.

I often illustrate this conceptually using a pretzel with three holes. The first hole is not the second hole. Neither is the second hole the third hole. But they are all tied together by the same dough. In other words, God the Father, God the Son, and God the Spirit all share the same divine attributes and characteristics while not being the same in their personhood.

Similarly, we witness the three distinct persons of the Trinity each taking a more prominently visible role in the ongoing narrative of Scripture at different times. Using the analogy of a newspaper, in the Old Testament God the Father is on the front page. His is the voice we hear from the most, and His are the actions we see carried out the most. In the Gospels, Jesus is front-page news. He is the superstar. We see references to God the Father, but Jesus is "above the fold."

Yet from the book of Acts onward, the Holy Spirit headlines. He's the One we get to know the most as He works with and through individuals and churches to take the power of God, the person of Christ, and the priority of the gospel to the world.

Transitions are always hard, and an impending absence makes them all the more challenging. Jesus knew this. He knew what His disciples were about to experience. In telling them about the Holy Spirit, He was trying to soften the transition ahead. He sought to assure them that even though He would no longer be with them physically, in His absence God would send Someone of the same essence. Someone so similar to Him that they wouldn't need to fear the gaping hole His leaving might produce.

Jesus even couched what He said in terms of endearment: "I will not leave you as orphans; I will come to you" (John 14:18).

Perhaps you know what it is to be an orphan. Or you know what it is to have parents who are absent emotionally or even to a large degree physically though not officially making you an orphan. You know what it is to grow up without the protection of parental covering and how vulnerable that leaves you to the wiles and lures of this world.

Jesus knew His disciples would feel abandoned when He left. They would feel as if they'd lost a parent or a coach or a guide. But He wanted them to know He wasn't leaving His followers in this evil, sick, sinful world to make it all on their own. He wasn't leaving them to the wolves. He would never do that to His disciples, nor would He ever do that to you and me. Rather, He left us all in the capable hands and heart of the Holy Spirit.

The Holy Spirit's role from that point forward was to act on Jesus' behalf just like Jesus acted on behalf of the Father when He walked on earth. He, the Holy Spirit, was sent to carry out the will of the Father and the Son among those who are saved. Just like each computer networked with others can read and interact with those others, the Father, Son, and Spirit, who all share the same divine nature, don't need to guess the will of the other two. Their awareness of one another's being and desires are innate within them as much as their awareness of their own beings and desires.

That's why you never have to worry whether the Spirit got the message when you've addressed your prayers to the Father. And you never have to wonder whether God heard, too, if you called out to Jesus. The triune God is so networked as one that they operate in sync at all times.

Yet just as the three distinct persons of the Trinity have unique roles to carry out, they also have unique characteristics—often highlighted or emphasized by "names"—that they demonstrate to us. And that finally brings us to the first name of the Holy Spirit we want to explore as found in Jesus' introduction of Him to His disciples—a name I'm sure you're familiar with, and the name I found I needed the most during the first years after my wife's passing: the Helper.

JESUS EXPLAINS

Jesus calls the Spirit the Helper. And He calls Him this four times in three chapters in order to seed both the name and the concept of

His work and presence into the hearts and minds of His disciples as well as into ours.

> I will ask the Father, and He will give you another Helper (John 14:16).

> The Helper, the Holy Spirit, whom the Father will send in My name, He will teach you all things, and bring to your remembrance all that I said to you (John 14:26).

> When the Helper comes, whom I will send to you from the Father, that is the Spirit of truth who proceeds from the Father, He will testify about Me (John 15:26).

> But I tell you the truth, it is to your advantage that I go away; for if I do not go away, the Helper will not come to you; but if I go, I will send Him to you (John 16:7).

Over and over again, we read that the Holy Spirit's role is that of a helper. The original word in Greek is *parakletos*. *Parakletos* is ripe with meaning, referencing one who is uniquely gifted to come alongside another and assist. When Jesus walked the earth, He came alongside the disciples to assist them in the various challenges they faced, even everyday challenges. For example, when they were hungry, He provided food. When they were tired, He gave them rest. And then when they experienced fear, He calmed their emotions. In moments of struggle, He gave them peace.

Whatever His disciples faced, Jesus provided assistance in facing it. But since He was leaving, they would no longer have His physical assistance nearby. Instead, they would have the help of the Holy Spirit.

Some English translations of Scripture don't use the word *Helper*. They use words like *Advocate* or *Comforter*. This is because the Greek term *parakletos* encompasses the Spirit's meeting all these "helping" needs, depending on the situation. God chose for the New Testament's inspired writers to define the Holy Spirit according to this particular name because it can fit a variety of circumstances and needs. It's a flexible term, so fluid that it more accurately reflects the Holy Spirit's ability to help us in times of need.

If you're depressed, the Holy Spirit can help you with encouragement. If you're discouraged, He can help you with new strength. If you're afraid, He can help you by calming your fears. If you're struggling, He can even ease the struggle. And if you're alone, the Holy Spirit can be your friend. He can flex to whatever situation you're in and whatever you need.

In fact, you may need Him one way today but in an entirely other capacity tomorrow. And that's okay, because this name—Helper—applies to all situations. He is God's provision in Jesus' place to meet you at your point of need.

What's more, *parakletos* assumes there is a problem and so there exists a need for assistance. It starts with the question, *How can I help you?* It starts with proximity to the problem at hand. It starts with presence. Because you can't help anyone in any real capacity from a distance.

YOU'RE NOT ALONE

The Helper Jesus introduces us to in this passage in the book of John is close enough to truly help when you need help the most. As we saw earlier in John 14:17, Jesus said, "You know Him because He abides with you and will be in you." The Holy Spirit is close enough to be with you in an experiential way. He is by your side, like a partner or a companion. Not only that, but He's also in you. This means the Holy Spirit walks *alongside* you while at the same time He makes His home *inside* you. And while you may feel alone at times in your life, this reality of the Holy Spirit's closeness to you both near and within means you're never truly alone.

Satan would like for you to forget that. He would like you to feel isolated and without help. And when you feel that way, it's easy to give up and lose hope. But when you remember the closeness of the helper

God has given you, you'll know you can get through anything life sends your way—without a doubt. You are not alone.

As a Christian, you have never been alone. From the moment you trusted in Jesus Christ for salvation from your sins, you received the companionship of the Holy Spirit both externally and internally. The reason He remains present in both locations is that, depending on the situation, you can need help in both areas of your life at the same time. Whether you're facing something in your external circumstances or struggling with internal thoughts or emotions, the Holy Spirit has positioned Himself to be available to you when and where you need Him the most.

THE HELPER AS COMFORTER AND ADVOCATE

Earlier I mentioned a couple of forms of spiritual help the Holy Spirit offers us—again, both names coming from the flex term *parakletos*: Advocate and Comforter. Let's talk about those.

The specific helping role I found myself needing from the Holy Spirit the most after losing my wife was that of Comforter. Not only did I feel alone in those early morning hours, sleepless nights, and evenings when the hands of the clock seemed to move so slow, but I needed comfort because of the pain I felt in my grief. I'm sure you've been in a situation where you needed this comfort as well.

Most of us have a cover we call a comforter on our beds, or at least close enough so it's available when we need it. A comforter is usually soft, somewhat weighted, and big enough to wrap ourselves in it completely, and it comes in handy particularly on a cold night or during a cold day. Comforters aren't used just when it's cold, though. I found myself using mine a lot after Lois's passing because I no longer had the physical warmth of her presence I'd come to know as second nature for nearly five decades. I needed a comforter every night in those first months, even if it wasn't cold.

The Holy Spirit as Comforter has come to give us the presence of God now that the presence of Jesus is no longer on earth. Whether we're going through a cold spell emotionally or spiritually—or even physically—the Comforter is close enough to reach out and wrap His presence around our hearts and souls in order to let us know we're not alone. Because Jesus has risen to the third heaven and no longer walks with us in the physical form on earth, the Holy Spirit has been assigned as a comforter for our times of loneliness and need.

Another name that can come from *parakletos* is *Advocate*. An advocate is someone who pleads your case—similar to what a defense lawyer does in a courtroom. When the Holy Spirit shows up as the Advocate in your life, He comes with the ability to defend you when accusations are made against you. He's there as an advocate for you when situations or circumstances stirred up by Satan are aimed at destroying you.

Legal advocates will always enter a legal system to intervene on behalf of the ones they're representing, and the Holy Spirit is no different. As the Advocate, He intervenes for us when we need Him to do just that.

THE SPIRIT'S NATURE

As we will discover throughout our time together in this book, the Holy Spirit can intervene in so many different ways because He's a non-material Being. Jesus came to earth as a material, physical Being. While here, He could go to only certain places and do only certain things simply because of the physical limitations allowed. Yet because the Holy Spirit is nonmaterial, He can be in all places at all times. He can be helping you at the same time He's helping me. He can be speaking to you the same time He's speaking to me. He can be advocating for you the same time He's advocating for me.

The Holy Spirit, as the third person of the Trinity, is not an "it." He's not just a "power" to turn on and use, although we'll later see that power is one of His attributes. He's a person present both alongside each of us and within us. And as a person, He desires for you to relate to Him as much as anyone else would want you to relate to them.

He also possesses intellect, emotion, and volition. He's not a robot where you get to push buttons and He obeys. He is not AI. The Holy Spirit exists as a relational Being formed of an immaterial essence in order to abide both with you and in you throughout your life.

One of the reasons we don't witness His help as much as we could is that we have relegated Him to robotic status. We've viewed Him as something to use, not Someone to know. If anyone in your life just wants to use you and clearly doesn't care about you, you know how your heart turns away from helping them. But that's often how we relate to the Holy Spirit.

We'll unpack how that affects His ability to help us in chapter 2, but my point here is that too often believers just want to use Him at will. And unless you and I truly understand and explore ways to relate to the Spirit and engage with Him, we will never fully experience the benefits He makes available to us.

The Holy Spirit can do so much. He can guide us. He can help us with our prayers. He brings things to our minds and helps us remember them. He teaches us. He convicts us. He strengthens us. He also searches the deep things of God and brings them to our awareness. And when He does, He can give us thoughts we weren't thinking on our own. He can give us ideas we didn't come up with on our own. He can make connections we never even knew to make or open doors we didn't even have the ability to knock on.

All of this takes place when we learn to "walk in the Spirit," as in an abiding relationship with Him.

WHAT DOES IT MEAN
TO ABIDE WITH THE SPIRIT?

The concept of abiding will come up in this book more than once, and I like to describe it by comparing it to drinking tea. Many of us have only a "visiting" relationship with the Spirit; we call on Him only when we're in trouble. When no problems are at hand, we don't relate to Him ongoingly. But to abide is similar to letting your tea bag soak in boiled water. When the tea bag abides in the hot liquid, the water takes on the flavor and nature of the tea. Yet when someone simply dips their tea bag in and out of the water, as so many of us do in our relationship with the Spirit, the tea doesn't have the opportunity to fully express itself in the water.

To abide with the Spirit means you're hanging with Him. It means He's involved in the totality of your life. You're connecting with Him all the time. That's why the Bible tells us to "pray without ceasing" (1 Thessalonians 5:17). It doesn't mean we're to get down on our knees and be in this physical posture of prayer at all times. Rather, it means we're to bring the Spirit of God to bear in all we do. Whether we're driving, working, shopping, or spending time with family or in entertainment, we're to be conversing with the Holy Spirit (praying) at all times. We are to talk with the Holy Spirit always.

When we operate in this manner, we keep the channel open to hear from Him where we should go, what we should say and how, and what choices we should make. Whether it's about a big matter or a small matter doesn't matter.

If you're serious about experiencing the work of the Spirit in the circumstances of your life, then it'll involve your intentionally abiding with Him. That's why Galatians 5:16 says we must "walk by the Spirit." Walking, last I checked, is an action, not a passive activity done to you. In order to walk, you must choose to move. You must move your legs. You decide on a direction, and then you go.

Similarly, you don't try to engage the Holy Spirit by passively acknowledging His presence. No, you are to walk with the Spirit. You are to move. You are to choose to connect with Him in an intentional way. And you go toward God by walking with the Spirit.

We will look at all that more closely in the pages to come, as well as how we engage the Spirit, but it comes down to putting your weight on your spiritual legs and exercising your spiritual muscles.

Now, sure, your spiritual muscles may have weakened over long periods of time with no real use. But just as you must use atrophied or strained muscles or ligaments in physical therapy *and keep using them*, you must use your spiritual muscles *and keep using them*. Only in their continual use will you strengthen their connection in your spirit to the Holy Spirit placed in you by God.

Walking is never about just one step; it always involves steps following steps. To walk with the Spirit is no different. It isn't just about reading a Bible verse a day to keep the devil away. It's an ongoing movement toward God through steps taken to pursue the Spirit's presence in your life. When you do that, you'll unleash the Holy Spirit's power in you in ways you never even imagined. You will tap into the abundance of all the Holy Spirit can supply.

As we continue to walk through these pages together, be intentional about your pursuit to come to know the Spirit and the character traits He exudes. Don't set this time aside as the last thing you get to…and only if you feel like it. Make knowing the Holy Spirit a priority. Abide with Him. When you do, He will give you the strength and increase the motivation and desire in you to keep going. Your relationship with the Holy Spirit is a two-way connection—you with Him and Him with you. Move toward the Spirit and watch what He will do.

2

THE DOVE

As we get to know the names and attributes of the Holy Spirit and how they each reflect His relationship with us in myriad ways, again, it's important to remember that He is a person to be known, not a power to merely be used. We often forget that because the Holy Spirit doesn't present Himself in a human body like Jesus did. But the next name we'll explore—the Dove—does give some manner of expression in a body, although not a human body.

In Luke 3:22, we read this: "The Holy Spirit descended upon Him in bodily form like a dove, and a voice came out of heaven, 'You are My beloved Son, in You I am well-pleased.'" The "Him," of course, was Jesus.

In this verse, the physician Luke tells us the Spirit appeared "in bodily form"—as a dove. This insight, given to us only by Luke as the other three Gospels don't mention the term *bodily form*, reveals that the Spirit can show up in our lives in physical form. He can take on the form of substance on earth, as a dove or a human being or anything else He desires to present Himself.

I had a little hint of this early in my grief process after losing Lois to cancer. While I carried the weight of loss all day long and throughout the evening hours, I especially felt the emotional drain and difficulty as well as the weight in the mornings.

I'll never forget one particular morning. I didn't have a lot going on because this was during the initial phases of the Covid-19 lockdown in 2020. My schedule was relatively empty, and I'd found myself in a very dull space, experiencing the pain of grief, when I got a phone call from a friend in North Dallas. He asked if he could bring lunch over in a few hours, and I accepted his kind offer.

When he arrived, he told me God had put me on his mind and heart in such a way that he couldn't shake it. He knew he needed to reach out, bring me something, and offer to pray for me.

Now, while my friend was and still is definitely a human being, I believe through him the Holy Spirit showed up for me that day. That was a "dove in bodily form" moment for me, right when I needed it the most. God has a way of knowing what we need and when we need it while simultaneously meeting that need through the ministry of the Holy Spirit as a helper, yes, but also, at times, as "a dove."

God chose a dove for Noah to send out in order to see if the waters had subsided after the flood (Genesis 8:9-12). When the dove came back, Noah knew there was no place for it to land. But the next time he sent out the dove, it came back with an olive branch in its mouth. That let Noah know the waters had subsided enough for vegetation to form. The dove came back to its familiar surroundings of the boat, but it brought with it a testimony of renewal for everyone there to see.

This is why we often see the image of a dove with an olive branch tied to events or discussions involving peace agreements or restoration. The dove symbolizes the end of judgment and the onset of a new day of blessing and freedom, reminding us that something new lies ahead when we're just coming out of a bad time. It's God's way of letting us know that while judgment may have taken place, renewal is now at hand.

We find a similar picture in the creation narrative. We read that as

God continued His creation of the world, "the Spirit of God was hovering over the waters" (Genesis 1:2 NIV). Like a dove soaring, the Spirit hovered in order to bring order out of the chaos beneath it. One of the reasons we should want a close connection with the Spirit, then, is that He can bring order out of chaos.

RESTING LIKE A DOVE WITH THE DOVE

Because doves are one of the most sensitive birds in God's creation, it's interesting that when the Holy Spirit descended on Jesus as a dove, it rested on Him. If doves come to bird feeders or trees in your yard, they're among the first birds to fly off when you walk outside. God, of course, knew about this sensitivity when He chose to descend to earth as the Holy Spirit in the bodily form of a dove.

For the dove to have felt free enough to rest on Jesus, then, says a lot. A dove won't get anywhere close to conflict, whether it senses it or witnesses it. A dove will land only where it senses great peace and safety.

Some time ago, when I was walking in Trafalgar Square in London, England, I met a man who was feeding the myriad pigeons there. You were still allowed to do that then. He held a bag of food, and like many other people in the square, he tossed the food out to the pigeons to watch them swarm it and eat it all.

As we talked, he said, "You know, you'll never see a dove here."

"You won't?" I asked in a tone that indicated I wanted to know why that was.

"No, you'll never see a dove in Trafalgar Square. It's just too chaotic and loud here. Too much movement." He continued, motioning to all the people milling around and all the pigeons flying about. "A dove couldn't function here at all. It wouldn't."

I understood what he meant. A dove desires peace. A dove hangs out in places that are serene. A dove doesn't linger or loiter in an agitated atmosphere. That's why it's significant that a dove descended on Jesus to symbolize the affirmation from the Father, resting on Him as the Father said, "You are My beloved Son, in You I am well-pleased" (Luke 3:22).

One of the reasons Satan seeks to keep us in a state of chaos is so the Holy Spirit won't function in full capacity. Rather than land and remain in the presence of that experience, the Holy Spirit will fly away, just as a dove would. This is because the Spirit's sensitivity rises, and He has to back away. Just like the Father doesn't abide in an atmosphere of disunity, the Holy Spirit doesn't abide in an atmosphere of chaos or sin.

The biblical image of a dove provides rest and calm. As David wrote in Psalm 55:6, "Oh, that I had wings like a dove! I would fly away and be at rest." This picture of the dove going away to a restful place stirs hope in our hearts.

It also reminds us that one of the reasons God often feels far away is that we choose to operate in an environment where His Holy Spirit isn't comfortable. This happens in our homes, marriages, friendships, churches, and work environments—and especially in our thoughts. When the environment reeks of chaos, confusion, and conflict, the Holy Spirit flies to where He'll be comfortable. His presence came down to "fulfill all righteousness" (Matthew 3:15), and that means he will not function where evil is prevalent.

If you want to experience the third member of the Trinity resting on you with His peace and His presence, you must create an environment where He will be comfortable. He must be at home in you, able to relax because His role is that of promoting and fostering peace. You can't have it both ways. You can't live fully in the Spirit while also living fully in sin. Certain conditions are necessary for the Holy Spirit to make His home in you, offering you the peace and presence you desire.

In Ephesians 4:25-32, we read about a few of these conditions necessary to foster a suitable environment for the Spirit to work:

> Laying aside falsehood, speak truth each one of you with
> his neighbor, for we are members of one another. Be angry,
> and yet do not sin; do not let the sun go down on your

anger, and do not give the devil an opportunity. He who steals must steal no longer; but rather he must labor, performing with his own hands what is good, so that he will have something to share with one who has need. Let no unwholesome word proceed from your mouth, but only such a word as is good for edification according to the need of the moment, so that it will give grace to those who hear. Do not grieve the Holy Spirit of God, by whom you were sealed for the day of redemption. Let all bitterness and wrath and anger and clamor and slander be put away from you, along with all malice. Be kind to one another, tenderhearted, forgiving each other, just as God in Christ also has forgiven you.

As you can see, we have the ability to "grieve the Holy Spirit of God." In fact, we can grieve the Spirit quickly. As you are aware, to grieve is to feel pain. To cry, feel sadness, and remain in a state of discomfort. Essentially, the opposite of what the Holy Spirit has come to offer us, which is peace, comfort, help, and joy.

BE MINDFUL OF CHOICES
INCONSISTENT WITH THE HOLY SPIRIT

One of the reasons many of us live in a perpetual cycle of discomfort is that we've alienated the Holy Spirit through our choices. Our thoughts, words, and actions have grieved the Holy Spirit within us. But because He's been "sealed" in us, which we'll explore in chapter 9, He can't fly off. He can't leave. Rather, He remains in a grieving state inside us, and this rises up within our own souls and spirits, manifesting in emotional, circumstantial, and spiritual chaos.

When the Holy Spirit is unhappy within you, how are you to be happy? When you have God's Spirit literally crying within your soul, how can you escape from feeling this pain and His tears? You can't. The

Holy Spirit's discomfort becomes your discomfort. But rather than address the trigger of grief within them, far too many people try to escape the unhappiness and the misery instead. They use entertainment, food, sex, drugs, spending, religion, exercise—you name it, anything they can use as a distraction.

The problem is they're trying to escape something the Holy Spirit can't escape. So no matter how hard they try, the Spirit's grief continues to resonate within until it bubbles over. The Holy Spirit is as sensitive as a dove and reacts quickly to what isn't consistent with His nature.

Several things inconsistent with the Holy Spirit's nature appear in the passage we just read in Ephesians. One of the first things is what we say. We read, "Let no unwholesome word proceed out of your mouth." If and when the Holy Spirit hears you speaking evil things, using unwholesome language, or issuing ill-intent with your tongue, again, He has nowhere to go. He becomes grieved within you—and you feel His grief.

Unwholesome words are defined for us more clearly in Ephesians 5:4: "There must be no filthiness and silly talk, or coarse jesting, which are not fitting, but rather giving of thanks." The bottom line is this: If you're cussing, the Spirit is crying. If you're tearing people down with your words, the Spirit is grieving. If you're telling jokes not designed to be funny but rather to be painful, aggressive, or derogatory, you've hurt the Holy Spirit. You've created an opportunity for the devil to set up camp in your heart and create greater havoc.

A lot of people open the door for the devil without realizing that's what they're doing. They do it through using poor judgment when it comes to speech. Whether through profanity, complaining, insults, or vulgarity, when their words are used unwisely, they set up a welcome sign for Satan.

When counseling married couples who can't get along, I'll often scratch my head. That's because after a few minutes of hearing them insult and blame each other, it's obvious they're creating their own misery. By grieving the Holy Spirit within them, they each wind up with a miserable relationship with the other.

What you say matters. How you say it matters. We are to use our words to build up and encourage each other, not to tear each other down. When we do the latter, tear down people made in the image of God, we're simultaneously tearing down the power and the peace-working presence of the Spirit within us.

Consider how you talk to someone from whom you're seeking help or a favor. Do you cut them down first? Do you say things you know will offend them? I imagine you instead say kind and encouraging words. We all understand this concept. Yet we often forget it when it comes to the Holy Spirit. We expect Him to jump when we say jump all the while offending Him with what we think, say, or do. Just like that approach wouldn't work in a human relationship, it doesn't work with the Holy Spirit of God.

The Holy Spirit, like a dove, is listening to your words. He's telling you to watch your mouth and be mindful of what you say. He's offended by putrid language filled with insults. The writer of Hebrews tells us that we are not to insult the Spirit of grace (Hebrews 10:29). God is insulted when He witnesses us using our tongues to hurt someone. If we're not careful or continue in this type of talk, we'll not only hurt others but will ultimately hurt ourselves as well.

In Southern Turkey lives a certain kind of bird—a crane. This crane mostly lives in the Taurus Mountains. When it flies, it cackles loudly, attracting the eagles nearby. The eagles trace the sound until they locate the source, and then they take off after the cranes to kill them for dinner.

The problem for the crane is that it was raised to cackle. It's part of its nature to do so. So the mature cranes have learned to carry a stone in their mouths to prevent them from cackling. And they pass this lesson on to their young. They no longer use their mouths to present an opportunity for their enemy to destroy them. The birds go about their business and arrive safely at their intended destination.

An "eagle" who doesn't mind a human or two for dinner exists in our spiritual realm. He's called Satan, and he has a keen sense of hearing. He's listening for what comes out of our mouths, and he likes it when we use them for evil. When he hears all of the cackling, complaining, and self-lauding, we've made ourselves prominent in his line of sight—and he sees it as a door of opportunity to ruin our lives.

We live in a day when unwholesome speech is almost part and parcel for everyday life. We hear words on television we never heard there in the past. We hear and read people insulting others in ways that would have caused a sailor to blush just a few decades ago. Twitter has turned into its own form of verbal war—a place where anyone can pretty much say anything to anyone without restraint or fear of repercussion.

The vitriolic speech has become so bad that we're becoming numb to it. We've begun to expect it. We're becoming comfortable with hearing it, laughing about it, or even using it ourselves. Vileness and filth have become so pervasive with regard to what we say or comment online that it no longer even shocks us.

But that doesn't mean they no longer shock the Holy Spirit. His purity and peace haven't changed. His standard hasn't lowered. His sensitivity hasn't become calloused. Anytime you or I entertain, accept, or participate in debilitating and unwholesome thoughts or speech, we grieve the Spirit of God and make Him cry.

It doesn't stop with our speech, though. As I mentioned, your unwholesome actions disturb Him too. And anytime you knowingly hurt someone, you're hurting the Holy Spirit as well. When you steal from someone, you're stealing from the Spirit. You're degrading the integrity of the Spirit. When you defraud someone, you're defrauding the Spirit. When you dismiss someone, you're dismissing the Spirit. Each of us is made in the image of God. To harm or marginalize anyone is to do the same to God.

First John 4:20 summarizes the connection between how we treat others and how we relate to God: "If someone says, 'I love God,' and hates his brother, he is a liar; for the one who does not love his brother whom he has seen, cannot love God whom he has not seen."

Instead of harming one another, we are to encourage one another. Instead of ignoring one another, we are to show honor to one another.

We are to be giving words of grace for each moment we face. We do this through encouragement, helpfulness, and also, as Ephesians 5:4 tells us, in the giving of thanks.

We live in a culture that not only allows hurtful speech and actions but seems to even endorse and perpetuate them. This reminds me of the little girl who was a pastor's daughter. She stubbed her toe and yelled "Darn!" Her dad didn't want to encourage that kind of reaction because the word *darn* was too close to an actual cuss word, so he approached her with a plan.

He told her that whenever she felt the need to yell out the word *darn*, she could tell him, and then he would reach into his pocket and give her a quarter if she showed the self-control not to say it.

The little girl smiled and looked up at her father as if a light had just come on in her brain. "Thank you, Daddy," she said. And then she added, "But I also know some words are worth a dollar!"

We're living in a time and a season when the value of clean speech has been lost. The price to speak morally and purely in our culture's mind has risen. We've entered the day of Isaiah 63:10, which says we no longer even try to abide by the Spirit but rather rebel against Him in what we say and do. It says, "But they rebelled and grieved His Holy Spirit; therefore He turned Himself to become their enemy, He fought against them."

Do you realize you can set yourself up in such a way that God will turn to act like an enemy? That's what Isaiah tells us. Our rebellions usher in God's response. When you choose to speak to people wrongly or treat them badly, you're asking God to fight against you. And He will do this just as any parent will rise up to defend their children who are being hurt by someone. God will rise up in order to block you or hinder you from harming others. He does this through the presence of the Spirit within you. Grieving the Holy Spirit doesn't stop with the Holy Spirit's cries. It evokes a response from God Himself to get things right within you.

Now, you can cooperate with this process or you can prolong it.

That's your choice. But whenever you make the Dove sad or grieve Him, you've positioned yourself in opposition to Almighty God.

What you and I want to do, rather, is seek to make the Dove comfortable within us. We want to make the Holy Spirit comfortable. We do this by creating an environment where He can function. We do this by refraining from participating in the divisions among us, whether it's cultural hate, racial hate, political hate, vaccination or non-vaccination hate… Whatever it is, we are to refrain from partaking in a culture of hate and division.

Satan stirs up this pot of hatred and division in order to cultivate an environment that makes it easy to reject people or put down those who don't live up to our standards. And while we may feel strongly about the issues facing our communities, nation, and world today, we need to be careful not to be pulled into the division through what we say and do. Or even through *how* we say or do.

Today's culture reminds me of the stories told about Winston Churchill, the UK's prime minister in the mid-twentieth century, and Lady Astor, the first woman seated as a member of Parliament. The division between these two individuals was so deep and intense that the stories strongly reflect that sentiment. After all, Churchill and Lady Astor were known for hating each other with a passion.

One day Lady Astor came into Parliament and saw Churchill. Just the sight of him made her angry, so she walked up to him and said, "Winston, if I was your wife, I would put arsenic in your tea."

Churchill looked up from whatever he was reading and responded, "Lady Astor, if you were my wife, I would drink it!"

On another occasion, Lady Astor ran into Churchill when he'd had too much to drink. He was obviously a little tipsy, so she took advantage of the moment and said, "Winston, you are an old drunkard!"

Churchill peered back at her—through blurred vision, no doubt—and replied, "Lady Astor, you are ugly. But at least I'll be sober tomorrow!"

As you can tell, these two truly loathed each other.

It doesn't take more than a few minutes on Twitter or other social media sites—or even in reading many YouTube comments—to see that the hatred between various groups of differing beliefs has reached the point of loathing. Anytime we have one group wishing for the deaths of another because they were either vaccinated or not vaccinated, we have sunk to an all-time low in our human existence.

You can observe other divisions—again, whether racial, political, class, or really, any other—and see the loathing is just as strong. When culture promotes such a spirit of disunity, particularly related to our speech, we as followers of Jesus Christ need to be careful not to fall into the trap of using our tongues to hurt others. When we do that, we grieve the Holy Spirit.

Not only that, but we reduce or even extinguish His work in our lives. We read about hindering the Holy Spirit's work in 1 Thessalonians 5:19, where we're told, "Do not quench the Spirit."

QUENCHING THE SPIRIT

Quenching the Spirit is similar to pouring water on a fire. The fire can no longer produce the warmth or benefit it was once intended to give. The flame has been put out.

Far too often we choose to quench the Spirit rather than respond to Him. When He has been grieved and creates discomfort within our souls (again, because we've been sealed in Him as Christians), we decide we don't want Him bothering us. We don't want Him convicting us. We don't want Him guiding us. So we pour water on the fire. We put the fire out.

In other words, we reject the conviction. We reject the teaching. We reject the leading. We reject the restraint. We choose instead to say whatever we want whenever we want and to whomever we want. We decide that telling others exactly how we feel in order to let it all out is more important than listening to and responding to the Spirit.

In essence, we tell the Dove to shut up because we're mad. We tell the Dove to leave us alone because we feel passionately about whatever issue we're facing.

Keep in mind that the Holy Spirit isn't asking us to stuff our emotions or never talk about what matters to us. But He is asking us to talk about what matters to us the way God prescribes. We are to be "speaking the truth in love" (Ephesians 4:15). If we don't speak the truth in love, we're fueling another fire—the fire of hatred, division, and conflict. As a result, even our prayers will become affected. James 4:3 says it like this: "You ask and do not receive, because you ask with wrong motives."

One of the most common reasons Christians don't experience answered prayer as much as they possibly can is they're living a lifestyle of conflict, whether conflict relationally with others, conflict internally due to a lack of alignment with God's truth, or conflict in what they say and how they say it. Conflict closes the door on prayer. That's because, again, the Spirit, like a dove, doesn't operate in an environment of conflict.

James explained the connection between conflict and our relational intimacy with God, especially the Holy Spirit, when he wrote, "Do you not know that friendship with the world is hostility toward God? Therefore whoever wishes to be a friend of the world makes himself an enemy of God. Or do you think that the Scripture speaks to no purpose: 'He jealously desires the Spirit which He has made to dwell in us'?" (James 4:4-5).

God has placed the Holy Spirit in every believer, and we have been sealed with the Spirit. This came at no small cost to our King, and yet we often treat the Holy Spirit like a side item. We dismiss His influence in our lives. As a result, God becomes jealous for the attention and closeness He has enabled each of us to have with His Spirit within us.

As we get to know the names and characteristics of the Holy Spirit more fully in this book, start building on that knowledge by resting on the Dove, the Holy Spirit.

IN SUMMARY

Just like the dove in nature, the Dove that is the Holy Spirit is sensitive. He is peace, calm, and stability. He's the opportunity to begin again, as was the dove of nature in the days of Noah. And because the Dove is sealed in you as a child of God, His misery will show up as your misery. His unhappiness will show up as your unhappiness. If you want to experience the peace, comfort, and calm the Spirit has to give you, you need to be aware enough not to offend or grieve Him.

Be aware of what you say and how you say it. Be aware of what you think and how it affects your behavior. Be aware of your choices with regard to what you see, read, watch, scroll through, or discuss. Be mindful of what grieves the Spirit, and then seek to reduce or remove those things in your life. That's when you'll begin to experience His presence bringing you the peace you long for.

Hanging out with the Holy Spirit can't be done if and when you choose to hang out with the world. You can't put both diesel fuel and unleaded in your car. You also can't listen to AM and FM stations at the same time on the same radio. It just doesn't work. Aligning with the world means not aligning with God's Spirit. You can't have both. But the good thing is it's up to you. Based on your free will, you get to choose. Will you cultivate closeness with the Holy Spirit by surrendering to God's ways? Or will you choose to make the Spirit miserable?

Whatever you choose will show up in your own emotions and life decisions. The Holy Spirit is positioned to bring you great hope, calm, power, and peace but only when you choose not to quench Him with how you live your life or what you say. God desires an intimate relationship with you. He is jealous for the Spirit's presence in you to connect with you rather than your connecting with the spirit of darkness, which is the world.

But again, it's up to you to choose. To choose to pursue this intimacy on an ongoing basis or not. But the Holy Spirit isn't a magic genie to be summoned with the snap of your fingers. He is sealed within you, available as you intentionally cultivate closeness through aligning with the truth and love of God.

3

THE LIVING WATER

Water is essential to life. When our bodies don't get enough water for their cells to function at optimum capacity, our health goes awry. Water is not an addendum. It's not an extra. It shouldn't be an afterthought. Water is core to living. And so is the Spirit in us through another one of His names and roles—the Living Water.

Physicians tell us to drink a lot of water on a regular basis so our cells are healthy enough to distribute the nutrition our bodies need in order to function. We're also told to drink plenty of water so waste and toxins can be easily removed from our bodies. Trust me, I know plenty about drinking water. After inheriting a lot of concerned "caretakers" after the loss of my wife, if I had a dime for every time someone in my family reminded me to "Drink water, Tony," or "Drink water, Daddy," I could retire and never work again. Sometimes I thought they were trying to drown me!

All joking aside, the world cannot exist without water. Human life, animal life, plant life—nothing here can exist without it. Our need for rain illustrates our desperation for it. With no rain—or at least not enough of what's required—everything becomes dry and eventually dies. Deserts, for instance, produce only animal and plant life able to withstand dryness, and only about a sixth of the world's human population lives in a desert region. Wherever our planet is without the water it needs, people, animals, and plant life are in dire trouble.

What physical water is to the body and to our planet, spiritual water is to the soul. If you starve the body of physical water, it won't work right. If you starve the soul of spiritual water, it won't work right. Just as physical water distributes physical life to the well-being of humanity, spiritual water distributes spiritual life to the well-being of our souls. When the soul is deprived of spiritual water, there will be deterioration and devastation in the life the soul embodies.

Jesus introduces us to this concept of spiritual water in the context of the Feast of Tabernacles. God had instructed the Jewish people to take part in this great feast in order to remind themselves of their journey through the wilderness.

QUENCHING SPIRITUAL THIRST

One of the more traumatic occurrences during that trip was their running out of water. Another occurrence was their seeming confinement when their enemies had them trapped at the edge of the Red Sea. Yet in both situations God had shown up for them in miraculous ways. At the Red Sea, He parted the water for them to cross to safety. In the wilderness, He let water gush out of a rock so they could quench their thirst. He also turned bitter water into clean water at another time so they wouldn't die of dehydration or water-borne diseases.

For the Feast of Tabernacles, the Israelites had been instructed to build booths, similar to what we call tents. They erected a tented city to live in during this feast, time established and set aside from the normal routines of life for the people to reflect on how God had supplied them through their greatest season of need.

Obviously, some of the provisions God supplied during these years had to do with water. Thus, it's fitting that at this feast, Jesus makes a statement that unveils this next truth symbol and character quality we'll learn about the Holy Spirit—Living Water. Jesus introduces the Spirit as "living water" in John 7:37: "Now on the last day, the great day of the feast, Jesus stood and cried out, saying, 'If anyone is thirsty, let him come to Me and drink.'" Jesus appeals to the people's very human need to quench thirst.

Living in Texas, as I do, can make this concept of quenching thirst very real. On those hot summer days when the heat index soars well above 100, it doesn't take long for dehydration to begin and the need for water to make itself known. The effects of high temperature and humidity signal the body that it needs a restoration of fluid—and soon.

When I used to run several miles a day for exercise, I always took along water to refresh myself as I ran. Any runner or jogger—even avid walker—knows what it is to be thirsty, as did the people to whom Jesus spoke when He introduced this concept. He used the illustration of the priests pouring water on the altar during the Feast of Tabernacles to let His listeners know He had come to provide spiritually for the souls and lives of the people the same way God supplied the Hebrews with refreshment in the wilderness.

It's easy to tell when our bodies are thirsty. Parched lips and a sluggish feeling alert us to our need to drink. It's equally as easy to tell when the soul is thirsty. The problem is that many of us have forgotten how to recognize and correlate these symptoms with a thirsty soul. But if you're living a life of discontentment, you have a thirsty soul. If you're living a life of confusion, you have a thirsty soul. If you're living a life of frustration, you have a thirsty soul. And if you're living a life of perpetual failure, you have a thirsty soul.

The soul's thirst makes itself known through dissatisfaction, discontentment, unforgiveness, rampant sin, confusion, internal chaos, and more. All of these manifestations are reflective of dry spots in the soul that are begging for water.

What's worse is that, just as we've tampered with how to quench the body's thirst, we've tampered with how to quench the soul's thirst.

When our bodies get thirsty, too many of us turn to options that don't actually satiate the body. We turn to a sugary soda or sweet tea or a chemical-based energy drink, yet physicians tell us they all fall short of the benefit of pure water. Whenever we substitute an illegitimate substance for water, we run the risk of negatively impacting our body.

Similarly, we often wind up drinking spiritual saltwater instead of the pure water Jesus came to give and the Holy Spirit supplies. Spiritual saltwater comes in the form of illegitimate relationships, illegitimate entertainment, illegitimate ego boosts, and more illegitimate "solutions." Anything that gives us a temporary lift to help us forget or cover how thirsty we really are just distracts us from what we need the most. Not only does it fail to quench our spiritual thirst, but it increases our need for spiritual water. Whenever something is awry in the soul and it goes unaddressed for a prolonged period of time, an even greater level of spiritual dehydration is produced.

Let this sink in: No saccharin or salty substitutes for the Holy Spirit's living and abiding presence in your soul exist. They just don't.

Because the need for spiritual water is so profound, it causes us to always be on the lookout for how to meet that need. And Satan likes to send us on chases or in circles aimed at locating cheap and bogus substitutes that were never designed to exist as authentic thirst quenchers. In fact, Satan doesn't mind if you confuse religion and spiritual ritual with the living water, because they will never meet your need either.

Only the Spirit offers you and me the living water of Christ, which we need for our souls to not only survive but thrive. This pure water is what will flush away the impurities that seek to control our every thought and every move.

Thirst is a conscious craving or longing of an empty soul. It reflects the reality of living in a spiritual desert. These are the dry times in our lives when we don't feel close to the Lord or in step with our spiritual goals. We feel like we're walking through that "dark night of the soul." And even though we're saved for eternity through the sacrifice of Jesus, we've forgotten to take advantage of all He came to supply to us while He was still on earth. If you'll look back at the first verse we read together, John 7:37, you'll see an action step Jesus said we're to take. I'll put it here for a reminder:

> **"If anyone is thirsty,**
> **let him come to Me and drink."**

Coming to Jesus is what you and I did when we came to Him for salvation. But the action we often forget once saved is that we still need to "drink."

When I preached on this subject at the church where I pastor in Dallas, I held a cup full of water as I talked about this passage. The cup was full. The water was pure. It had cost me nothing to procure. But it also benefited me nothing until I took the action of intentionally drinking it. Just holding the water would do nothing for me. Just talking about the water would do nothing for me. Even smelling the water would do nothing for me. Not until I drank the water would my body be refreshed and my physical needs met.

It's a simple illustration, but its meaning is profound. You and I can have water freely given to us but still remain thirsty. We can possess spiritual water but still remain unsatisfied. Possessing and drinking are two very different things. To drink of the spiritual water Jesus came to supply through the Spirit means you and I must appropriate this living water into the internal operation of our lives.

If you've accepted Jesus Christ for salvation so you're bound for heaven when you die, that's good. Actually, that's great. But you must not allow that eternal security to lull you into complacency while on earth. Eternal salvation isn't sufficient for healing and satiating a thirsty soul during your journey as a human being. To do that, you must come to Jesus and appropriate the living water He offers into your daily existence. And when you do, this living water becomes more than just something you have access to; it becomes something you're using and benefiting from.

OUR ACTIVE RESPONSIBILITY

Because we have neglected to emphasize the role and responsibility of our own participation in appropriating this life-giving water, I want to illustrate it another way as well. I really want you to comprehend how critical you are in this process of utilizing all that the Spirit has for you. This is not a passive relationship where you sit back and the Spirit does all you want Him to do for you. You have an active role to play in your sanctification as well as in your satisfaction on earth.

On Thursdays where I live, a waste disposal company sends a truck to our neighborhood, and its workers pick up the trash I've taken to the curb. They do this for all of the homes in my area. We pay a small fee, and this service is enacted. I'm sure you have some similar service.

But what I want to ask you is this: When have the trash-removal employees ever come to your door and offered to empty your trash inside your home rather than requiring you to take it to the curb? Or when have they ever knocked on your door because you forgot to set your trash out on time?

Like for me, they probably have never done either of those things for you. In order to have our trash removed, we have to take it to the curb. We have to bag it and set it out by a designated time. And depending on where we live, we even have rules about how many trash containers we can set out, how full they can be, what items are excluded, and when recycling bins are allowed.

Some of us are waiting on the Holy Spirit to come and pour the living water down our dry throats. But Jesus tells us we need to come to Him and drink. We need to intentionally set out to drink. We can't blame God for our thirst when He has supplied the way to quench it. We can't point fingers at others when our lives are in shambles yet we refuse to drink of the living water offered to us in the Spirit. We can't insist that everyone else flex to our needs, desires, and wants in order to assuage the emptiness we have inside when Jesus has told us all along how to meet our spiritual needs.

Spiritual water is internal work that only you can do within your soul. If and when you experience a craving of discontent welling up within you or notice spiritual issues unresolved, you need to drink of the living water available to you. Only then will you be refreshed once again.

Notice, though, that Jesus doesn't say you should come to Him for information. He doesn't say the Holy Spirit will provide you with Google-like search results on thirst, dehydration, purpose, or related topics you may want to know about. No, while the Spirit is our teacher and instructor, as we will discover later in this book, Jesus begins by saying we must come and drink.

Anyone can learn about the Bible, theology, religion, or any spiritual matter only to remain thirsty. This is because knowledge without relationship is never enough. If you ever went on a blind date, you know the information you were given beforehand—no matter how impressive—wasn't enough to already know whether you'd want to go out with that person again. The only way to know was through relating and abiding with that person for an amount of time. Impressive information can quickly dissolve in person.

God doesn't want to solely be an information center for your mind. If all you wind up with is information about a potential date, you haven't actually had a date. God wants to be a life-giving, personal experience for your heart.

When you and I come to Jesus and drink through our faith and belief, we receive this living water activated within. Jesus explained this process to us, as John reports in John 7:38-39:

> Jesus stood and cried out, saying "If anyone is thirsty, let him come to Me and drink. He who believes in Me, as the Scripture said, 'From his innermost being will flow rivers of living water.'" But this He spoke of the Spirit, whom those who believed in Him were to receive; for the Spirit was not yet given, because Jesus was not yet glorified.

WATER THAT FLOWS

What God wants to do is place a pump inside your soul that will produce ever-flowing water. It's running, living water designed to keep your life, thoughts, and heart fresh with the Spirit's leading and love. Water that doesn't move grows stagnant; it becomes ripe for bacteria to grow. That's why the Spirit exists as *flowing* water. As Jesus described it, that which will "flow rivers of living water" will be within you.

Flowing water is designed to go through every aspect of your innermost being, nourishing, feeding, and refreshing each one. To understand the necessity of this, it's important to remember that you are not your body. Your body is merely a vessel, or a mechanism and avatar, to facilitate your soul. You are your soul.

When you die, your soul leaves the body and enters eternity. Your body stays here because you are not your body. All your body does is provide you with a host to function within while your soul walks the earth. What your soul wants to do is enacted through your body. Your soul is your ID. It's your personal signature of existence.

You can think of it like a code uniquely assigned to you as your identification. And when you die, this code remains with you. You remain as your soul. Your existence is your soul. Your body is merely designed to function in the physical world through the exercise of your five senses. Your body can hear, touch, see, smell, and taste. As a result, your soul can function on earth. Your true identity—your personhood, your soul—sends signals to your body so it knows what to do.

The problem is that our souls have been scarred. Everyone's soul has been scarred. When you were born, you entered a world filled with sin. But even before you were born, you inherited spiritual transfers of decay through your human identity. This only becomes exacerbated through life. Whether other people's sins and choices affect us or our own, or even just the general atmospheric sin of this world order, our souls, to varying degrees, take on the damage that surrounds us.

People who have very deep soul damage may wind up doing hideous things to themselves, scarring their bodies. Perhaps scarring others' bodies as well. Perhaps they do this in an effort to numb pain. But a scarred soul cannot heal a scarred body. Regardless, many of us spend an enormous amount of time and energy seeking to fix a body with an unresolved soul. Yet anytime an unresolved soul exists, the body simply finds a new way to express the pain within it.

That's why behavior modification techniques typically last only so long. If you're holding back a bad behavior but you haven't dealt with the soul damage that contributed to that behavior, the soul will simply find another way to express its damage elsewhere. Only when we allow the life-giving refreshment of living, flowing waters to move through us do we remove the toxins of the soul and heal the damage done within. When we drink, or abide, in a close relationship with Jesus, His stream of water produces life in us through the presence of the Holy Spirit.

While your body is designed to communicate with the physical world and your soul is designed to communicate with yourself, God has given you a third element of being in order to communicate with Him—your spirit. Now, Scripture tells us that because of sin, we're spiritually dead when we're born (Ephesians 2:1). It's our nature from the beginning. That's why our spirit needs to be made alive, which is what happens when we accept Christ for salvation.

THE SOUL'S EFFECT FROM INSIDE OUT

When you receive Christ, God places a pump inside your human spirit otherwise known as the Holy Spirit. Through Jesus, the Holy Spirit invades your human spirit and gives you spiritual life. The Spirit resides in the soul. The soul resides in the body.

As the Holy Spirit pumps living water into your spirit, which then overflows into your soul, it offers you healing, contentment, order, strength, and purpose. Your soul then begins to give new information to your body.

This new information, or directive, is in alignment with the truth of the Holy Spirit. As a result, your body begins to do things differently.

Your body begins to say and do that which glorifies God and brings good to others. And as long as the Holy Spirit is free to release His living water into your spirit, which then feeds your soul, which then directs your body, you will continue to heal and produce that which is good.

In our homes, we have plenty of water piped in through an elaborate delivery system. Yet even though we have access to this water, we can keep it from flowing into our homes. All we have to do is close the main water valve. But when we do, we won't have the water we need to wash our dishes, flush our toilets, brush our teeth, take showers, and much more, cleaning away what could harm us.

Some of us have been so messed up in our souls for so long that we've forgotten how to open the valve allowing the living water to flush out the garbage within us. Our bodies have become so contaminated because we don't have the living water to wash, flush, or cleanse us, to offer us what we need.

Your soul cannot be healed until you allow the living water of the Spirit to flow. You must release the water within and drink. When you do, the innermost water will transfer from the Spirit to your spirit, to your soul, and ultimately to your body.

In the Bible, the prophet Isaiah communicates these words from God: "I will pour out water on the thirsty land and streams on the dry ground; I will pour out My Spirit on your offspring and My blessing on your descendants" (Isaiah 44:3). The emptiness, discontent. and dissatisfaction born out of sin can be addressed only through the Spirit of God. God gives us His blessing by nourishing our dry and barren souls through the provision of the Spirit.

When Jesus said He came to give us life and life more abundantly (John 10:10), He was talking about life beyond the treadmill. He was referring to life off the grid. He wasn't talking about the kind of life where we, like mice, keep spinning the wheel in endless loops only to wind up going nowhere at all. Jesus came to give the kind of life that gushes with meaning, contentment, and satisfaction. He does this through the presence and life-giving water of the Holy Spirit—life that starts from the inside and then moves out.

GLORIFYING JESUS

When Jesus told us about the Spirit, He hadn't yet been glorified. He was still in His physical form. The Holy Spirit came after the resurrection. He came on the Day of Pentecost, and everyone was filled with the Spirit at that time. This coming of the Spirit took place when the disciples decided to both privately and publicly glorify Jesus. That's how you and I keep the pump of the Holy Spirit working freely in our own lives. Because the Spirit came to glorify Jesus (John 16:13-14), so must we.

And as you know, Jesus came to glorify God. Thus, when we use our lives to glorify Jesus, we are also affirming what Jesus came to do, which is to glorify God. When that is done, the Spirit empowers and enables more living water to flow within us.

Asking for the water won't keep the water flowing. Understanding the water won't keep the water flowing. Acknowledging that the water is there won't keep the water flowing. Only by your bringing glory to Jesus Christ through your words and deeds does the Spirit kick in within. That's why anytime you marginalize Jesus, even though you believe in God and speak freely about God, the work of the Spirit is simultaneously marginalized in you. The Spirit of living water is energized when Jesus Christ is privately and publicly exalted in your life.

Experiencing the full manifestation of the Holy Spirit in your life is closely tied to how you interact with Jesus. Many Christians just visit Jesus. They go to church for a Jesus-visit. But then they go about their lives until the next time for a visit. But visiting Jesus on Sunday is not abiding. That's called checking off an item on a list. Only an abiding relationship with the Lord will produce living water that flows in you at a level that will bring you life. The more the Spirit sees you glorifying

Jesus, the more He will pump the water so that it flows into your soul and transforms your body.

WHEN THE WATER
FLOWS THROUGH AND OUT

When you need the living water to heal, cleanse, or refresh you, you need to set loose the Spirit within. You do this through identifying with and abiding with Jesus. You do this through privately and publicly bringing glory to Jesus. When Jesus is glorified, the pump comes on and the transformation takes place. What's more, all of this takes place for free. It doesn't cost you a dime. Revelation 21:6 and 22:17 say:

> Then He said to me, "It is done. I am the Alpha and the Omega, the beginning and the end. I will give to the one who thirsts from the spring of the water of life without cost."

> The Spirit and the bride say, "Come." And let the one who hears say, "Come." And let the one who is thirsty come; let the one who wishes take the water of life without cost.

You get the living water at no cost. Why? Because the cost has already been paid. It's been placed inside of you through the work Jesus Christ did on the cross. The deliverance you desire is already in you. The guidance you desire is already within you. The grace you desire is already within you. You just need to drink. And when you do, you'll begin to notice the changes taking place outside of you.

One of the ways you know the living water is flowing inside you is that other people start to notice it. They start to comment on how you've changed for the good. What's more, they start asking what you've done, because they want to experience life transformation as well.

I've found a main reason some people are so mean to others is that they're really messed up in their souls. They don't know how to be nice anymore. As a result, they cuss out other folks or do things to harm them. They no longer want to serve anyone but themselves. They find service to self far more gratifying than service to others. As a result, they run empty. They become spiritually dehydrated. They no longer share any good with others because they no longer have any good within.

Yet when you have the life-giving flow of the Spirit in you, flowing freely throughout you, it can't help but gush out and cause others to desire what they see in you.

When I was a young boy growing up in Baltimore, Maryland, we knew we could always go swimming on Saturdays—at least a form of swimming. That's because on Saturdays the fire marshal opened up the local fire hydrant, water gushed out, and we had a temporary water park in the hood. I'll never forget running through the water barefoot, having a great time playing with my friends.

I was puzzled by how a fire hydrant shorter than me could have all that water coming out of it every Saturday, literally for hours. So I asked my daddy to explain. He told me the hydrant didn't hold the water; it was just a mechanism through which the water flowed. A reservoir in Druid Hill Park held the water, and a pipe beneath the ground connected to the reservoir.

My father went on to explain that when the fire marshal came around, all he did was open up the tap, making it possible for an abundance of water to come pouring through. Without that connection, the fire hydrant would sit empty.

That reality fascinates me now as much as it did then. Now, because it's such a clear illustration of what the Holy Spirit does in and through us. No matter how big we are or how much influence or fame we have, a simple connection will do. What matters is the reservoir. When we tap into the reservoir of the Holy Spirit, the water will not only flow but continue to gush out as long as we keep the tap open.

We keep that tap open by glorifying Jesus Christ both privately and publicly. We keep it open by abiding in His presence. We keep the water flowing by aligning our hearts with God and allowing the Spirit's presence to produce His character within us. When that happens, other people as well will benefit from the life-giving water that not only flows in us but flows through us.

4

THE ANOINTING

You may still be wondering how much benefit there is to studying the Holy Spirit's names and attribute descriptions. But again, the benefits come about as you get to know His various functions and roles. His names and how He's referenced or described in Scripture indicate His work.

Again, keep in mind that God, the Father, was the point person in Old Testament times. Jesus, the Son, became the point person on earth during the period of the Gospels. And the Holy Spirit is the point person now, during this time we call "the church age." He's the third member of the Trinity, assigned to act on our behalf while we are on earth and to help us do the work God desires to be done here.

The Father functions from the third heaven, and the Son sits at His right hand to rule spiritually from heaven to earth. It's all carried out through the Holy Spirit. His role is the most prominent from all members of the Trinity in the church age. And yet as I mentioned in this book's Introduction, He's often misunderstood, marginalized, misused, underappreciated—and even forgotten.

That's why I'm hoping our time together will encourage us all to focus more fully on the Spirit and what He's doing in and through us. The more we engage with Him, the more power, peace, and purpose we tap into in our lives.

This next name for the Holy Spirit we'll explore—the Anointing—is found in 1 John, chapter 2. I encourage you to read the entire passage from verses 18-29, but for our purposes in here, I'll quote only from verses 20-21 and 26-27:

> You have an anointing from the Holy One, and you all know. I have not written to you because you do not know the truth, but because you do know it, and because no lie is of the truth...

> These things I have written to you concerning those who are trying to deceive you. As for you, the anointing which you received from Him abides in you, and you have no need for anyone to teach you; but as His anointing teaches you about all things, and is true and is not a lie, and just as it has taught you, you abide in Him.

If you've been in church for any length of time, you've heard the words *the anointing* or the phrase *the anointed one*, and in this chapter, the Holy Spirit's name is the Anointing. This term speaks to a specific work of the Holy Spirit you certainly don't want to leave home without. It's a key feature of the Spirit's work in our lives.

For many people, the concept of the anointing boils down to an emotional experience—when they feel something tied to a spiritual thought or situation in church, in prayer, or at any time, really, and believe it's the anointing. This can take place when a preacher delivers a great sermon or a worship leader performs a great song. It could come during the reading of Scripture or during personal prayer time. Oftentimes when people talk to me after church, I'll hear comments like, "That was an anointed sermon, Pastor," or "You really had the anointing today, Pastor."

More often than not, what those individuals are referencing is that they experienced an emotional reaction or an emotional impact based on what they heard.

While the Spirit does create anointed moments in ministry, I want to caution you to not relate every emotional reaction to a belief in the anointing. Many people—whether preachers, singers, or even podcasters—elicit an emotional response simply with their own talents. Or your particular emotional response could be tied to something you're going through at that moment. While the Spirit does show up in these experiences, I also think people often limit the anointing to emotional reactions rather than coming to understand that the anointing goes much deeper.

The anointing involves more than emotion. It involves the deep work of the Spirit in someone's life. In Acts 10:38 we read how Jesus' anointing empowered His work:

> You know of Jesus of Nazareth, how God anointed Him with the Holy Spirit and with power, and how He went about doing good and healing all who were oppressed by the devil, for God was with Him.

In Luke 4:14-20, we also read of the attachment of the anointing to tangible, physical work:

> Jesus returned to Galilee in the power of the Spirit, and news about Him spread through all the surrounding district. And He began teaching in their synagogues and was praised by all. And He came to Nazareth, where He had been brought up; and as was His custom, He entered the synagogue on the Sabbath, and stood up to read. And the book of the prophet Isaiah was handed to Him. And He opened the book and found the place where it was written,
>
> > "The Spirit of the Lord is upon Me,
> > Because He anointed Me to preach the gospel

to the poor.
He has sent Me to proclaim release to the captives,
And recovery of sight to the blind,
To set free those who are oppressed,
To proclaim the favorable year of the Lord."

And He closed the book, gave it back to the attendant and
sat down; and the eyes of all in the synagogue were fixed
on Him.

We can see that the anointing involves much more than emotion
in these passages. It's the inner-working of the Spirit that enables and
empowers the outer-working of tangible good works, which glorify
God. And if even Jesus functioned according to the anointing within,
how much more should we?

What you need to remember about the anointing, though, is that
you already have it. Every Christian has the anointing. If you're saved
and trust in Jesus Christ for the forgiveness of your sins, you possess
the anointing within you. You own it. It's there. You don't have to go
looking for it. You don't have to be baptized into it. And you don't have
to cross off a certain number of items on a checklist in order to gain it.

You have the anointing. It's a gift from God. The anointing speaks
of the indwelling presence and work of the Holy Spirit in your life.

First Corinthians 6:19 states it like this: "Do you not know that
your body is a temple of the Holy Spirit who is in you, whom you have
from God, and that you are not your own?" The Holy Spirit indwells
you.

In the Old Testament dispensation, the Holy Spirit would come
and go. He would visit a person or situation, do His work, and then
leave. But in the New Testament and ultimately in the church age,
Jesus gave us the Holy Spirit as a permanent resident in our lives. His
anointing is nothing that sits outside of us. It is within. And it is con-
stant. In fact, you can't be a Christian and not be anointed. If you're a
Christian, you're anointed.

Now, you may not know how to use the anointing you have, but that doesn't mean you don't have it. You do. The key is knowing that you do and creating intentions to use the anointing in such a way so as to benefit from it.

GETTING THE MESSAGE

One of the benefits the anointing can produce in you is to illuminate God's messaging to you, both from His Word and from His heart. The Holy Spirit's role is to take the thoughts of God and show them to you while you walk the earth. The job of the anointing is to give you the data from heaven so you know how to best operate based on it in history.

Yet if you don't know you have it, you won't use it. You won't benefit from it.

Unfortunately, today far too many Christians don't know they have the anointing. Thus, they don't know how to use it, and as a result, they fail to maximize any benefits from it. The reason we have so many problems with our bodies and the outer workings of our lives is that we have infection in our souls, and the reason we have infections in our souls is that we have human spirits contaminated by sin.

Only when the anointing enters and expands within the human spirit does the human spirit become perfected and pure. The Holy Spirit's anointing feeds the human spirit the information and data it needs to distribute to the soul, which then sends it to the body. The body then functions differently, and our outward lives become more in alignment with God when we intentionally pursue the anointing's influence within.

We all have a perfect resident within our human spirit. As believers, we have the Holy Spirit's anointing. But we must learn to allow the Spirit to guide, direct, and infuse our lives with His anointing. When the Holy Spirit is free to invade our human spirit, our soul gets healed. Thus, if you want to fix your body, you first have to clean up your soul.

And if you want to clean up your soul, you have to start getting the right information from your spirit. You have to open the pathway for the Holy Spirit to speak to your spirit by intentionally pursuing and accessing the anointing within.

When your soul gets disinfected due to the expression of the human spirit that's been permeated by the anointing of the Holy Spirit, it tells your body what to do, your mind what to think, your ears what to hear, your eyes what to look at, and your legs where to go. Your soul does all of this because it has received pure information from the Holy Spirit on how to function in alignment with God's will.

Many of us have dimmer light switches in our homes, designed to bring the light in a room up or down, brighter or dimmer. When the dimmer switch is turned off, there's no light at all. When the dimmer switch is low, there is limited light. But when it's turned up to capacity, there is maximum light. God has given every believer a dimmer switch called the anointing. It's the role of the Holy Spirit to progressively bring the light of God's truth into your life.

Now, you may choose to keep this dimmer switch off, which means you won't have access to any of the light of God's truth. Or you may keep it turned low with the light of God's truth coming to you only dimly. But if you want to experience the full expression of God's truth—and His love—turn the dimmer switch up to its maximum level. This will enable you to see from God's perspective.

The anointing is quite literally the divine messaging you've been qualified to receive since the Holy Spirit entered into your human spirit. But it's up to you how much you tap into it in order to utilize it. You're authorized to receive it all. But no one will force you to do that. You have to make that choice.

THE NATURAL MAN, THE SPIRITUAL MAN

I'd like to ask you to read 1 Corinthians 2:9 all the way through 1 Corinthians 3:3 every day this week, because this passage is pregnant with life-impacting truth, and verse 9 stands out to me regarding our study on the Holy Spirit.

> Just as it is written, "Things which eye has not seen and ear has not heard, and which have not entered the heart of man, all that God has prepared for those who love Him."

This passage isn't talking about heaven. It's not referencing what we'll experience in Glory. It reminds us of all we have access to while on earth. Yet we know only what God has prepared for those who love Him when we intentionally pursue and access the Spirit's anointing. When the anointing is turned on and the dimmer switch is turned up, you're free to see things normal human eyes can't see. You get to hear things normal human ears can't hear. You get to think things normal human minds can't even fathom.

In other words, the anointing takes you beyond the veil of the physical world. It shows you what your eyes can't see. It allows you to hear what your ears can't pick up. It lets you perceive that which you wouldn't normally think of on your own. It pulls you from the physical realm into the spiritual realm so you can perceive, experience, see, and sense that which is from God Himself.

Never forget that if all you see is what you see, you don't see all there is to be seen. If you live limited to your five senses, then you'll never access all God has in store for you. All that means is that your dimmer switch to the anointing is either turned down low or completely off. You must access the ability to see beyond the physical realm through your connection with the anointing.

The passage in 1 Corinthians goes into greater detail on how this works. We read a little of this insight in chapter 2, verses 10-13:

> To us God revealed them through the Spirit; for the Spirit searches all things, even the depths of God. For who among men knows the thoughts of a man except the spirit of the man which is in him? Even so the thoughts of God no one

knows except the Spirit of God. Now we have received, not the spirit of the world, but the Spirit who is from God, so that we may know the things freely given to us by God, which things we also speak, not in words taught by human wisdom, but in those taught by the Spirit, combining spiritual thoughts with spiritual words.

The anointing of the Holy Spirit is like a God-based search engine, because He searches the very depths of God. He's the Google engine of God. He's like a deep-sea diver going into the abyss of God's thinking and heart in order to transfer God's thoughts into your life as His follower. In this manner, you tap into the spiritual thoughts that exist beyond your physical senses. The very job of the Spirit is to reach into the mind of God and transfer His thoughts, sights, and desires to believers. His role is to take truth and turn it into your experience by bringing truth into your reality.

He doesn't do this for information's sake; He does it for transformation. What's more, all of this is free. We've received it, as the passage tell us, "so that we may know the things freely given to us by God." It doesn't cost you a thing. Once you accept Jesus Christ, these thoughts of God are free to you. Wisdom is free to you. Wisdom exists when the Holy Spirit combines spiritual thoughts with spiritual words. The Spirit dips into the mind of God and brings to the mind of humanity these spiritual thoughts and spiritual words, which is the truth of Scripture. That's what the anointing is.

Issues arise when we rely too heavily on our own nature rather than on the anointing within. As the following verse to the passage above states—verse 14—"But a natural man does not accept the things of the Spirit of God, for they are foolishness to him; and he cannot understand them, because they are spiritually appraised."

Let me put this another way: The non-Christian lives without the anointing. He is a "natural man." And because of this, the truth of God appears as foolishness to him. But what's more, as we will see later in this passage, when you or I as a believer in Christ refuse to tap into the anointing within, we can also be deceived into thinking that the things of God are foolishness.

But in this initial grouping of the "natural man," Paul is referring to those who don't even have access to the Holy Spirit's anointing. Like a home without cable, the ability to tap into the programming from above is completely absent. Without that ability, try as they might, they cannot access it.

But a second group with access to the anointing is found in this passage. We see it in verses 15-16:

> He who is spiritual appraises all things, yet he himself is appraised by no one. For who has known the mind of the LORD, that he will instruct Him? But we have the mind of Christ.

The natural man does not have a receiver to be given the wisdom of God. The spiritual man has the receiver, but he must keep the receiver turned on. Then the spiritual man can appraise and evaluate all things through a spiritual grid. You are a spiritual Christian only if you consistently send all of the data you receive through a spiritual grid.

Another way people describe this is "living according to a Christian worldview." The grid, or the worldview, is how you filter what you see and hear and experience in order to provide you with context and discernment. When you keep the dimmer switch turned high and access the anointing of the Holy Spirit within, then everything you take in will go through the spiritual grid. The spiritual words of Scripture will combine with spiritual thoughts producing in you "the mind of Christ."

People who live with the mind of Christ think the way Jesus would think. They process information the way He would processes it and empower our obedient response to it. The Holy Spirit enables this kind of living because He has the ability to bring Jesus' thoughts to our brains.

The third group referenced in this passage is that of a spiritual man who has not taken advantage of the anointing within. Unlike the natural man who doesn't have access to the wisdom of God, this spiritual man has access. But he simply refuses to use it—or uses it sparingly. We read in 1 Corinthians 3:1-3,

> I, brethren, could not speak to you as to spiritual men, but as to men of flesh, as to infants in Christ. I gave you milk to drink, not solid food; for you were not yet able to receive it. Indeed, even now you are not yet able, for you are still fleshly. For since there is jealousy and strife among you, are you not fleshly, and are you not walking like mere men?

In this third group, the life of the believer appears not much different from that of the natural man since they both walk like mere men. Even though the ability to receive God's wisdom exists, this group of people chooses not to use it. They've moved the dimmer switch all the way down or even off. As a result, they don't gain access to the heavenly programming from above and are therefore limited to living their lives apart from divine assistance.

WHAT'S PROGRAMMING
GOT TO DO WITH IT?

A lot goes into how well we're able to receive from the anointing. One of the best ways I know to explain it has to do with our cable programming on earth. I have Direct TV in my home, and to get it, I have a receiver in my bedroom as well as one in my den. They're both designed to receive programming from a satellite in the sky.

Now, as you know if you also have Direct TV or some service like it, this receiver allows me immediate access to hundreds and hundreds of stations I can pull down into my television, based on my viewing taste. Whether it's drama, history—or much to the annoyance of those who may be visiting my home, the news—I've got access to it all.

But I recently ran into a problem getting the programming I was used to. I would turn on the receiver, but it would fail to produce a picture on my TV screen. I checked whether my receiver was plugged in, and it was. It's just that for some reason my receiver and my television were no longer talking to each other.

That's when I decided to do what I always do when I run into a technical problem: I called my daughter Chrystal to come over and help me. Chrystal understands all of the idiosyncrasies that go into technology. So she came over and brought her brother Anthony with her. When I told them about my problem, they went into the den, where Chrystal recalibrated my connection. Suddenly, the television screen that had issues for longer than I'd like to admit was now working. Chrystal fixed it simply by reconnecting the TV and my source.

God has programming in heavenly places He wants to bring down into your earthly existence. As a born-again believer, you have the receiver to access that programming. But if you're living your life as a fleshly minded Christian, your connection to the receiver isn't calibrated. You won't get the picture offering you guidance, wisdom, and governance for your life to show up.

See, just because you possess the anointing doesn't mean you automatically get to experience the anointing. You get to experience it only when you align your spirit with the Holy Spirit according to the ways and the values of the Spirit.

God has programming for your life, thoughts, family, finances, career, mental stability, church, and even for our society. But if and when you're not synced with Him, you won't be able to access any of it.

What's interesting to note is that when Paul wrote to the Corinthians in the passage we just looked at, there had been a five-year gap from his first visit to his letter. That means the individuals he said were still "fleshly" had already been saved for five years. Yet even after that length of time, they were walking like a natural man. Paul admonished them because, after half a decade, they should have been more spiritually mature. In essence, they'd wasted five solid years of spiritual growth potential.

In fact, in the book of Hebrews, the writer condemns those Jewish Christians who had been saved as far back as the beginning of the church some 30 years earlier yet still didn't know how to walk according to the anointing within (Hebrews 5:11-12). This is a stern warning for all of us, because no matter how long a person has been in church, or read the Bible, or participated in spiritual rituals, the anointing role of the Holy Spirit must be intentionally pursued and applied. Without it, spiritual growth will not take place. At most, you'll have behavior modification for a time, but the old ways and the old thoughts will creep back in if and when you operate on a base system rooted in human wisdom.

ABIDING

As we saw in the opening pages of 1 John 2, the anointing is accessed through abiding. Again, abiding is a theme that will keep popping up as we continue to explore the role of the Holy Spirit throughout this book. That's because abiding is the key way to tap into all the Holy Spirit has in store for us.

You and I must do more than visit the Spirit. We must do more than attend church on Sundays. We must abide in His presence, pray without ceasing, and seek to align our hearts and minds with God's viewpoint on every subject based on His Word. If your first question when issues arise is not *What does God say about this matter?*, then you are not abiding. And if God's perspective is the last place you go, you're contaminating the truth of God with lies.

Abiding is a lifestyle. Accessing the anointing is a lifestyle. God does not desire weekend visitation from you. He wants you to live with Him all the time. When that takes place, you will have turned the dimmer switch to high, enabling the programming from heaven to reach you and thus illuminate your mind and your thoughts with heavenly wisdom.

And then you won't need anyone to teach you from a secular, non-Christian perspective. As you agree with God's revelation, the Holy

Spirit will give you divine illumination so you can experience personal transformation. You won't need anyone to explain things to you based on human wisdom. You'll already know the truth. You'll be able to see things as you ought to see them, through spiritual eyes. As the psalmist writes, "Open my eyes, that I may behold wonderful things from Your law" (Psalm 119:18). You will come to understand God's Word for yourself when you fully access the anointing within you.

Like the servant we read about in 2 Kings 6:14-17, God will open your eyes so you can see the spiritual army all around you. When you can see what's going on in the spiritual realm, your fears will dissipate. Your anxiety will fade. Your need for control will release itself in surrender to God. When you live spiritually, you get to see things spiritually.

God is always in the midst of what's going on. We just can't always see Him because we've become so used to using our physical senses rather than tapping into the Spirit's anointing in us.

Far too many of us are being attacked physically or emotionally yet don't know what to do because we don't know how to view things spiritually. All we see is what we see. But when all we see is what we see, we can't see what God is doing. God exists in the spiritual realm, and the Holy Spirit pulls back the scales from our eyes so we can witness that truth for ourselves.

You have access to Him right now. You have access to spiritual sight right now. That access has been given to you through the anointing within. But it's up to you if you choose to use it. This means you must reject human wisdom that conflicts with God's Word. Then you must act on the truth of God as revealed in Scripture. The Holy Spirit will then clarify and empower your understanding and experience of God's truth in your life.

5

THE LORD

Before we talk about how we find the Spirit's strength in His next name—the Lord—let's talk about an infection called indwelling sin. It's never pleasant to talk about it, but it's necessary.

I'm sure you'll never forget the onset of the COVID-19 pandemic. Most people can remember where they were when they first became aware of just how severe the virus was and what we were being asked to do about it.

I happened to be in Las Vegas filming a Bible study when we got word that all hotels there were closing their doors, and ours gave us only a few hours' notice to pack up and get out of Dodge. While I continued filming the Bible study, my assistant was on the phone with the travel agent looking for flights. We must have changed reservations a half dozen times as they were canceled or rescheduled.

My children were concerned about my well-being, and so during breaks while filming the study, I was on the phone with them. We didn't know how COVID-19 spread or how quickly it spread. We only knew that the world was seemingly shutting down overnight. Car rentals were no longer an option, and the idea of renting a bus even came up.

Come to find out, I actually was sick. I wasn't feeling well, and I had a slight cough and some energy depletion. The day after arriving home, I would be diagnosed with walking pneumonia and successfully treated for it, but in the meantime I didn't know what was wrong. All I knew was a virus was on a rampage, especially targeting people my age.

Yet I knew people all over the country and around the world must be frightened, and so I needed to do what I'd been called by God to do—preach His Word in season and out. So we ran around Vegas the rest of that day filming a message of calm in the midst of chaos to send out to our listeners on social media as well as for the Bible study sessions.

As we did, I had to whisper the same message of calm to myself at times. Upheaval and feelings of being unwell can unsettle anyone, me included. But thankfully, we made it out that night, even after filming the entire Bible study and the special social media message for our listeners and viewers on the fears associated with the lockdown. We got on the last flight out of the city to Dallas with only minutes to spare. But we got out. And we made it safely home.

As you know, in the weeks, months, and even years to follow, the world focused on finding a way to curb the spread of this virus. Millions of people lost their lives. I contracted it twice myself. Maybe you contracted it as well or know someone who did. Despite all of our best efforts, the spread continued as the spread of viruses often do.

Here's where I'm going with this: The COVID-19 virus isn't the only virus that has run rampant through humanity. Another virus has infected every man, woman, boy, and girl ever born. In fact, there is no person in the human race who hasn't been infected, and thus affected, by the virus known as indwelling sin.

When you and I were born, we not only picked up genetic strains that are part of our DNA from our parents, but our parents also transferred a sin nature to us. A sin nature is a nature prone to rebel against the standard of God. It's woven within our very human nature so that there's no real way to extract it when life is formed. This sin nature has transferred its damaging effects to our souls, which then manifest outside our bodies through the words or actions we take part in.

That's how all of our souls have become so distorted. Anytime a virus infects a host, it can cause irreparable damage. In the case of sin, the soul becomes so distorted that the body winds up doing what it was never originally designed to do in both word and deed. The consequences of these words and actions then lend themselves to influencing a cycle of destruction and decay.

As we've already seen, your body simply does what your soul tells it to do. Your soul tells it to do what your human spirit allows and encourages. And since the human spirit has been infected from conception with the indwelling of the sin nature, we have a world of people doing all manner of evil on earth.

A question then lends itself to be answered just as the question of how to slow the spread of COVID-19 consumed us for so long: How do we address the sin infection within us all?

Now, most of the time we answer that question by trying to manage the infection within. We try to stifle it or isolate it so it doesn't fully express itself. That's why we spend so much time teaching and disciplining our children. We're aiming to give them ways to manage the sin nature within them. I call this external reformation rather than internal transformation. We merely attempt to camouflage the sin within through the way we look, the money we have, the car we drive, the place we live, and so on. We try to hide the fact that we've been infected.

But despite our attempts, the virus keeps showing up. It shows up in uncontrolled anger. It shows up in judgment or pride. It shows up in words we chose and should not have chosen. It reveals itself in addictions. It makes itself known through emotional pain, discouragement, or even depression that dominates our hearts and minds. Our distorted souls distort our view of the world around us, thus causing us to create havoc with our own words and actions.

If you've ever been to a carnival or amusement park, you may have come across the traditional house of mirrors, where the mirrors distort what they reflect. They're shaped in such a way that they make you look extremely tall, wide, small, or lopsided. Your physical body takes on a whole new shape and look based on the mirror reflecting it.

Similarly, a distorted soul leads to a distorted self-image that produces distorted words and actions that damage lives. Of course, this distortion is expressed at different degrees and levels of intensity, but it's expressed by all of us no matter how hard we try to mask it.

All of that is tough news to swallow, but God has good news. He's provided all we need to address the sin operating within our flesh. As you might imagine since we're focusing on the Holy Spirit in this book, the solution to our sin problem lies with the Holy Spirit.

We read about this in 2 Corinthians 3:17-18:

> Now the Lord is the Spirit, and where the Spirit of the Lord is, there is liberty. But we all, with unveiled face, beholding as in a mirror the glory of the Lord, are being transformed into the same image from glory to glory, just as from the Lord, the Spirit.

Notice the words *but we all* in the passage. These three words are very important, because they indicate no exceptions exist. That said, you are not an exception. God's solution is perfect for anyone who will use it. No matter what you may have thought, said, or done, God can turn your life around when you tap into the power of the Holy Spirit. The Spirit has the strength to address the damage done to your soul from your childhood, exacerbated by your circumstances and then irritated by your own actions.

TRANSFORMATION AND LIBERTY

And so we find the Spirit's strength as we uncover another of His names—the Lord. Now, you may think this is an odd name to call the Holy Spirit since Jesus is frequently known as Lord. But that's why it's important to truly study the Holy Spirit. We have far too frequently relegated Him to one role—that of emotionalism, all the while ignoring or downplaying His myriad other roles.

Jesus Christ is no longer physically on earth; He is physically in heaven. But if you're a believer, He is spiritually in you. Yet we often forget that in this process of Jesus taking up residence in each of us spiritually, He does so through the agency of the Holy Spirit.

The Lord is the Spirit. And as we saw in the passage earlier, "where the Spirit of the Lord is, there is liberty." The term *liberty* indicates release from anything or anyone holding you illegitimately hostage—whether a relationship, a habit, an attitude, a belief, or a situation. Whatever it is, you need to realize that you have the Spirit, who is Jesus the Lord, inside of you to release you. A release mechanism is operating inside you because where the Spirit of the Lord is, there is freedom to be found.

The Spirit of the Lord releases you from bondage through one specific strategy: He transforms you from the inside out. In the last verse in the passage we read above, we see that we're each being transformed into a new image. This image reflects the Lord. God's goal for each of us is not external reformation. It's not even virus management or contagion reduction or infection containment. God's goal is spiritual transformation.

The only way you know you're growing in your Christian life is that you're changing. If you're not changing, that indicates you're not growing. That's true no matter how loudly you may be shouting in church or how much time you may be spending in your prayer closet. Until there is visible, demonstrable, what God calls transformation, spiritual development isn't occurring. The infection is still operating within you. You're still sneezing. Your nose is still running. Your cough is still debilitating, in a spiritual sense. Nothing has changed if there's no internal healing through transforming.

The release mechanism to free you from sin's bondage kicks in as you're being transformed from the inside out. As your human spirit becomes more amplified by the Holy Spirit within, it begins to penetrate the soul and address the infection of indwelling sin that manifests itself in our flesh. As that infection is addressed by this expansion of the Spirit, the soul gives new data to your body. Your body then responds with actions more in alignment with God's own reflection. You're experiencing changes on the outside because you're being transformed on the inside.

Understanding this, and how it works, is the key to kick-starting the process of becoming a better version of yourself as well as setting yourself free from the bondage of sin. If you're unable to change the physical manifestations of sin's impact in your body despite all of your best attempts, it's because there hasn't been enough expansion of the Spirit of the Lord within. Where the Spirit of the Lord is, there is liberty.

In contrast, where the Spirit of the Lord is not, there is darkness and bondage. We see this contrast explained earlier in 2 Corinthians:

> Their minds were hardened; for until this very day at the reading of the old covenant the same veil remains uplifted, because it is removed in Christ. But to this day whenever Moses is read, a veil lies over their heart; but whenever a person turns to the Lord, the veil is taken away (2 Corinthians 3:14-16).

As long as people choose to live without the abiding presence of the Spirit of the Lord within, Jesus Christ made real through the person of the Holy Spirit, a veil will remain over their hearts. God hardens the minds and covers the hearts of those who remain fixated on the law rather than on Jesus. The old covenant does not set a person free. Only the Lord can do that.

That's why apart from the presence of the Lord within you, reading the Bible is no better than "reading of the old covenant." The Living Word gives birth to the written Word inside you through His work of the Spirit. You can go to church and hear a sermon yet leave unchanged.

This is because a veil blocking the Word from doing its work in you exists. The old arrangement doesn't work in the new reality.

When a new U.S. president is inaugurated, an administrative shift occurs. In other words, the new president brings in a new one as the old one is removed. A covenant can be compared to an administration. In the Old Testament, God operated according to the rules and bylaws of the old covenant. But in the New Testament and beyond, He operates and relates to us in an entirely different way. Whereas in the Old Testament and the old covenant, the Holy Spirit would come upon people to empower them or guide them, in the new covenant era, the Spirit dwells inside of people.

In the old covenant, David prayed that God would not take His Spirit from him (Psalm 51:11). He knew what it was like to live without the presence of the Spirit, so he fiercely desired the ongoing abiding of God's presence. Yet in the new covenant, the Spirit continually abides within believers. He has been permanently placed inside each of us, and it's an entirely different way of operating. Yet many people are still stuck in the old way. They're stuck in the law, regulations, and rules of the old. They're trying to manage their souls rather than set them free.

This reminds me of how I was told my great-grandmother got clothes clean. Probably similar to your great-grandmother's work, she would scrub and scrub and rub and rub each piece of clothing on a scrubbing board and then scrub some more. Entire cultures in our world today still do this. It gets the clothes relatively clean, yes, but it doesn't give them much chance to last long.

Today, we have washing machines in America. We don't have to use scrubbing boards. Our clothes are gently washed on a spin cycle and then dried in yet another machine (unless hanging clothes on a line out in the sunshine is still your preference). This washing action not only gets them clean but allows them to last for years rather than the few months they might last when put through the wringer of a scrubbing board. While the old way and the new way have the same goal, they don't use the same method.

I don't know about you, but I'm glad we have washing machines. I imagine you prefer yours to the old way of using a scrubbing board as well. We prefer the washing machine over the scrubbing board because the washing machine gives us more power with less effort.

The beauty of the new covenant, the Holy Spirit's work in the human spirit, is the built-in power you and I now have to address the stains on our souls. Because the Spirit of the Lord now indwells within us, He allows us the opportunity of gentle adjustments and gentle cleansing in order to create a clean heart and pure soul. This new arrangement is designed to release each of us while simultaneously making us clean both internally and externally.

LIFTING THE VEIL

Just like there's a certain way to get a washing machine running, there's a certain way to approach spiritual transformation. According to the passage we just looked at, you must approach this process with an unveiled face. More so in the past than now, when a woman got married, a veil would almost always be covering her face when she started down the aisle of a church. The veil was there to camouflage a full and clear view until she reached the church altar. Her unveiling there was to be a special moment between her and her husband-to-be.

As a pastor, I've performed many wedding ceremonies where the bride has worn a veil, and there's always a point in the service when the veil is lifted, usually by the groom rather than the bride herself or perhaps her father. Almost without fail, those attending the wedding let out a collective "Ohh!" They do so because they behold the bride's beauty. They can all see her clearly.

The passage we read earlier reminded us that the old covenant included a veil. Even though the law was read and applied, God had placed a veil over the hearts and minds of those who did not yet possess the indwelling of His Spirit. Not until a person came to the Lord, who is the Spirit, and received Him inside, would the veil be lifted. Lifting the veil not only enables the person once behind the veil to see more clearly, but it exposes all that was once covered. Lifting the veil involves a willingness to be fully exposed.

You can't come to God and be transformed if you come in a spirit of lies and deception. You can't come to Him pretending everything is okay and you're not nearly as bad off internally as He knows you are. You can't come to God "faking it until you make it." You can only come to Him raw, exposed, and unveiled. For transformation to occur, pretending must stop. The pretending you do with yourself, the pretending you do on the job, the pretending you do at church or with your spouse, family, or friends—all the pretending you do must stop if you want true transformation to set in.

God desires that when you come to Him, you remove the veil. You lift the camouflage. You wipe off the makeup. You reveal your true self. Since the Holy Spirit is called the Spirit of Truth (John 14:17; 15:26; 16:13), He can only do His own transforming work when we deal with Him authentically and biblically.

After all, pretending never helps anyone in a doctor's office. If you go to a physician and act like everything is okay when it's not, the doctor may not run the appropriate tests to diagnose what's really going on. And without a timely or accurate diagnosis, the doctor can't treat you to make you well.

We understand this when it comes to seeking medical attention, but somehow we forget it when it comes to seeking spiritual healing. In order for God to address whatever is causing you to be spiritually ill, you must unveil yourself to Him completely. Just as you would in a doctor's examination room, you must give Him full access. For God to uncover and heal, you must stand before Him raw and unveiled.

The moment you cover up, hide, lie, deny, or act with any other form of pretending with God is the moment you declare your lack of desire for true healing to take place. It doesn't matter if you're reading the Bible, praying, attending church, or going to a small group. If you do any of that without an unveiled face, you're not seeking true and radical change.

Coming clean with God is how He can make you clean within. You need to be honest with Him. This will affect the way you pray and what you say. This will affect the way you interact with Him—and with yourself. Taking the veil off exposes the areas of infection within so God's Spirit can be free to address them. You are to come to God as beholding a mirror that will reflect His glory and attributes in you. If that mirror is covered, it won't reflect much of anything at all.

In biblical days, people didn't use glass mirrors because they hadn't yet been created. They used polished brass. Now, polished brass is a mirror, but it's not at all like a glass mirror. In order to use a polished-brass mirror, people had to first shine the brass, then hold it up and move it around to get the light to hit just right to see themselves. It took a bit of time to play with the brass mirror until they got the reflection they wanted to see.

In other words, they had to work at it. It wasn't as simple as pulling out a pocket mirror and seeing their reflection. A lot of variables had to come together in order for them to behold an image in the mirror at all consistent with the image in real life. So when the illustration of a mirror is used in the Bible, it means much more than just a simple reflection. It involves the work and conditions that produce the reflection as well.

We get a taste of what this work might be when it comes to our own spiritual transformation in James 1:19-21:

> This you know, my beloved brethren. But everyone must be quick to hear, slow to speak and slow to anger; for the anger of man does not achieve the righteousness of God. Therefore, putting aside all filthiness and all that remains of wickedness, in humility receive the word implanted, which is able to save your souls.

It's critical to note that James is writing these instructions to Christians. We know this because he opens by addressing them as "beloved brethren." So the people he's talking to already have souls that are saved. That's important to realize, because it helps us pick out the distinction when he says the things he asks them to do will be "able to save your souls."

IMPLANT

Another way of looking at this would be to use the term *deliver*. By doing what James writes in this passage, a person isn't saving their soul for eternity. That salvation has been sealed through Christ's atoning work. But when these instructions are carried out, the soul within gets saved, or delivered, from the contaminants and distortion of sin. We do this by receiving the Word that's already been implanted.

The implant James talks about here is the Holy Spirit operating in your human spirit. The implant exists. But just as a human body can reject an organ transplant or medical device implant, you must receive the Word for the implant to bear fruit and bring the life it's intended to bring you. The implant of the Holy Spirit is hungry for the nourishment of the Word. The Spirit can receive this nutrition when you take the Word seriously by receiving it. James shows us what it means to receive the Word in the next few verses:

> Prove yourselves doers of the word, and not merely hearers who delude themselves. For if anyone is a hearer of the word and not a doer, he is like a man who looks at his natural face in a mirror; for once he has looked at himself and gone away, he has immediately forgotten what kind of person he was. But one who looks intently at the perfect law, the law of liberty, and abides by it, not having become a forgetful hearer but an effectual doer, this man will be blessed in what he does (verses 22-25).

To be transformed is not a passive action that happens to you. You don't just sit back and the transformation takes place. To have the infection of your soul dealt with, you must first come to God with an unveiled face and then come to the mirror of His written Word, the Bible.

LOOKING IN THE MIRROR

You must position that mirror so that the light of God's Spirit shines on it, revealing the truth you need for personal transformation. When you hear this truth, you are then to apply it. As James writes, you are to "prove yourselves doers of the word, and not merely hearers who delude themselves."

When James references the "he" looking at a mirror, he uses the Greek word for "male." It's not the word that means all of humanity, whether male or female. I imagine he does this because he knows how men look at mirrors. Once in the morning is usually enough to last us all day, just long enough to shave and comb our hair.

But women in general often use mirrors more intently. Some hang out with as many as six mirrors, meandering through them each day to ensure everything looks just right—their hair, their makeup, their clothes. Forgive me for having a bit of fun with this, but mirror number one is the bathroom mirror they stare into when they first wake up. That shows them how messy things like their hair got overnight.

Their second mirror is called a vanity mirror. This is where they go next to address what they saw messed up in the bathroom mirror.

After the vanity mirror, they pull out a hand mirror to look at angles they couldn't see in the vanity mirror.

Then there's mirror number four. This is the full-body mirror, where they look at their outfit and shoes and turn around to ensure everything looks great.

You've probably guessed that the fifth mirror is on the visor in their car, or sometimes it's the rearview mirror. But it doesn't stop there, because the sixth mirror sits snugly in their purses to be pulled out whenever any of the previous five mirrors aren't around.

Of course, this is one reason women usually look great while men appear with their hair sticking up or bits of food in their teeth!

When James says we're to be like one who "looks intently at the perfect law, the law of liberty, and abides by it, not having become a forgetful hearer but an effectual doer"—*intently* is the key word. He uses this illustration to emphasize the point that if your soul is going to be changed, saved, or delivered, you must intentionally come to the Scripture with an unveiled face—a face you've seen as it really is—and apply its truth in your heart.

This then will bleed into your actions. You will become a doer of the Word, because the transformation within will lend itself to outward obedience. You'll want to obey God's Word rather than just feel obligated to obey it. We are to read and meditate on His Word until we see how it applies to our own issues.

Far too many people read the Bible merely to determine how it applies to others. They read it so they can judge others or hold them to a standard they don't even subscribe to for themselves. But God wants you to look at the Word like a woman might look in a mirror. You are to abide in it until you see your own reflection connected to it. Only then will you even know what needs to adjust for the truth. You're to hang out in the mirror of the Word until you become fully exposed. Our new nature is hungry for the nutrition of the Word.

The mirror brings reality into focus for you. It shows you what's wrong. It shows you what needs to adjust. It shows you what is real, like mirrors are designed to do. When you approach the Word of God as a mirror for the Spirit to use in your life, you're no longer just reading a page. You're reading about your own personality exposed in the Word. The Spirit of the Lord brings you freedom from bondage and deliverance from spiritual death by illuminating the Word in your spirit, which then nourishes your soul and positively affects your body.

We are not to live as hearers of the Word only. Each of us must be an effectual doer. Just as the term *Lord* is given to someone who typically governs another, the Word is to govern our spirits within. The Word is to influence what actions we take. The Word promotes and produces growth as we gaze into it and abide in it through the power of the Spirit.

If you're not changing or maturing spiritually in your walk with the Spirit, you're either not coming to God with an unveiled, honest face or not allowing the Word to mirror your own life and reveal it. When you're able to do both of those things consistently, the changes take place internally. The Spirit of the Lord frees you up to live more like Christ in your actions, attitudes, character, and conduct. You begin to resemble Jesus as you go through your life.

After all, that's the Spirit's goal. He's been given to us so we may glorify Christ. The Holy Spirit abides in us so we might know what it means to truly surrender to the Lord of lords and King of kings in all we think, say, and do. You will progressively be transformed from glory to glory, that is, from one level of spiritual development to the next. You will be set free to be everything you were designed to be.

When a woman is pregnant, it shows. Her appetite changes. Her mood changes. Her body changes. It shows because life is growing on the inside. When you receive the Word implanted within you, when you abide and allow it to do its work in you, it will also show. What you choose to do for entertainment will change. What you say will change. Even your emotions and your mood will change. Everything will change because of the new life growing on the inside.

And just as a woman relies on physical intimacy to create the new life within her, the Holy Spirit relies on spiritual intimacy to do the same. It's in the closeness and authenticity of your relationship with the Spirit of the Lord that the liberty you've been desiring all this time will grow within you. The Holy Spirit entered you at the conception of your salvation. But for the Spirit to grow within, you need to hang out with and be intimate with the Word of God in such a way that it reveals you to you and produces the spiritual growth you need and desire.

6

THE WINE

Before we explore this next name for the Holy Spirit—the Wine—let's talk about sleep.

We all know what it's like to be startled out of sleep by an alarm on our phones or when the radio's been set to suddenly turn on. We know how it feels to be awakened from an unconscious state to a state of conscious reality. Sometimes that happens at what seems like the most inopportune time. We're deep in sleep and enjoying the rest our bodies need. We're not ready to get up. We don't want to get up. But the alarm was set because we knew we would need to wake up.

Whether by the sound of an alarm or the gentle touch of a spouse, we're awakened to let us know it's time to get going. It's no longer time for lying around, hanging out in bed, tucking ourselves under the covers. There's a world in which we must now be activated to participate in it. It's time to wake up.

Paul had a concern when he wrote to the church at Ephesus—a concern about their ongoing slumber. He knew they needed to be roused from their sleep. Even jolted out of it. They needed to wake up to the new spiritual reality in which they lived and functioned.

The Christians at Ephesus lived in a predominantly pagan culture, a society clearly anti-God. The culture did not respect their values, and its people certainly didn't operate according to divine guidelines. They did not view themselves as needing to be acclimated to any kingdom worldview other than their own individual kingdoms.

Yet in the midst of the mayhem set loose in Ephesus lived this group of believers who had made the radical choice to trust in Christ for salvation. They had set out on a pathway to become transformed. But unfortunately, they fell into a spiritual stupor if not an unconsciousness along the way.

That's why throughout his letter to the Ephesians, Paul keeps pointing them back to recognizing that they don't function from a place on earth. He keeps reminding them that they now operate from heavenly places. He's trying to help them see that a spiritual sphere from which they need to learn how to carry out their lives exists. He urges them to live with this kingdom mindset and worldview, which will shape their decisions.

We read his attempts to rouse them in Ephesians 5:14: "For this reason it says, 'Awake, sleeper, and arise from the dead, and Christ will shine on you.'" Paul is concerned that the followers in Ephesus are spiritually snoring. They're focused on the physical to such a degree that they've come to disregard the spiritual altogether. The culture has lulled them to sleep, dulling their spiritual perceptivity.

Unfortunately, what was true of Christians in Ephesus is similarly true of Christians today. Far too many believers are spiritually asleep. They're asleep to the kingdom orientation we are to live by. Their senses are tuned in to the secular world along with all of its stories, intrigues, and drama. And as a result, we have entered a season when much of our society is the walking dead. We're part of a spiritual zombie world, because anytime people function in the physical without a proper orientation to the spiritual, they will function as the dead.

This world order is run by Satan, and his goal is to keep people spiritually cut off from the source of life, God Himself. What's more, he's had some practice and has become very proficient at it.

Paul sought to combat this spiritual attack on new believers by trying to help them become more acclimated to spiritual truths. One of the primary spiritual truths he aimed to share with them involved the Holy Spirit and His role in helping saints live out a kingdom life in a secular land. He wanted the believers awake, because he knew that in this absenteeism, slumber, and snoring of Christians, Satan is successful at keeping us ineffective kingdom influencers.

The same is true for us today. We must wake up. We must hear the alarm clock of heaven, or we will only continue to be ineffective at impacting the world for God and for good.

BE WISE AND WAKE UP

In Ephesians 5:15, Paul urged, "Be careful how you walk." He wasn't talking about their gait; he was referring to how they walked through life. He warned them to be careful to maneuver through this life "not as unwise men but as wise, making the most of your time, because the days are evil" (verses 15-16). He wanted them to stop wasting the time they'd been given. To stop killing time. To stop living lazy. He urged them to instead make the right kind of decisions that would bring God's light into a darkened world. Paul knew it then as we know it now. The reason he wanted this was because the days are evil.

Make no mistake, we live in an evil world. Evil surrounds us on every corner. Jesus defeated Satan at the cross, but Satan has still been given a long leash from which to operate on earth until Jesus' final return. To say that Satan has made the most of that leash is an understatement. Much to the detriment of so many worldwide, he's put on a party.

We don't have time to lie around in our perpetual states of ease. Instead, we must do what Paul urged next: "So then do not be foolish, but understand what the will of the Lord is" (Ephesians 5:17). We must understand what God's will is so we can enact it. We must learn how to look at life from God's perspective so we're fulfilling His purposes not only in our individual lives but also as a Christian collective. God desires to work both in and through us for the betterment of others and the advancement of His kingdom agenda on earth.

But we can't do that until we wake up.

Paul explains the process of waking up in the next few verses of this chapter by contrasting something most human beings can relate to—the drinking of alcohol—with the experience of being filled with the Holy Spirit.

Now, if you don't drink alcohol, at least not to the point of drunkenness, you can still probably relate to this illustration based on witnessing how other people act when they're drunk. I'm sure you've seen someone drunk in a movie, in a play, or just out in the general public.

In Paul's day, drinking was a popular thing to do, so he knew his listening audience would relate to what he had to say. We read it in verse Ephesians 5:18: "Do not get drunk with wine, for that is dissipation, but be filled with the Spirit."

And now we come to this chapter's name for the Holy Spirit—the Wine.

Paul compares what happens when a person drinks too much wine to what can happen when we're filled by the Spirit. He encourages each of us to become spiritually full or intoxicated by the Spirit rather than becoming full or intoxicated from alcohol.

When you and I become full of the Holy Spirit, He is free to influence our thoughts and behavior. In a similar way, when a person is drunk on wine, it's obvious that the wine is influencing what they say, how they say it, how they walk, the choices they make, and much more. You really don't have to look too hard at someone drunk to figure out what the dominate influencer is in that moment. You know the person is drunk because they're acting outside of their normal processes.

For instance, when police officers pull over drivers they suspect are drunk, they will often conduct a sobriety test. Part of that test is determining if the drivers can walk a straight line. If they are truly drunk, they won't be able to walk the line. They'll weave or stumble or both. Alcohol has impacted their behavior.

What Paul wanted to illustrate through this comparison with wine is that the filling of the Holy Spirit should also impact behavior—though, of course, for good. It should be obvious to those around us that we're spiritually intoxicated. If and when we become so overwhelmed with the filling of the Spirit that we no longer function according to our normal, sometimes not-so-good processes, everyone will be able to see the change in us. The filling of the Spirit is designed to produce discernable behavioral differences.

Filled with the Spirit, your views ought to be different. Your standards ought to be different. Your words definitely ought to be different. Even your courage to carry out God's will ought to be different. If you'll recall, at the Day of Pentecost in Acts 2, the people thought Peter and the other disciples had had too much to drink. They thought they were drunk.

> But Peter, taking his stand with the eleven, raised his voice and declared to them: "Men of Judea and all you who live in Jerusalem, let this be known to you and give heed to my words. For these men are not drunk, as you suppose, for it is only the third hour of the day; but this is what was spoken of through the prophet Joel: 'And it shall be in the last days,' God says, 'that I will pour forth of My Spirit on all mankind'" (verses 14-17).

Peter explained to the onlookers that what they were seeing was real. The changes in the men and how they spoke were profound. But those changes weren't due to alcohol; they had to do with the pouring out of the Spirit of God on them.

This same Spirit given to the disciples at that moment in time is in you. As a believer in Christ, you have received the Spirit. But to possess the Spirit is not the same as being under the influence of the Spirit. He is there, sure. But He may not be in control. You have to release control to the Spirit for Him to fill you.

SIPS OF THE WINE WON'T DO

God wants all Christians to be living under the dominating influence of the Holy Spirit. The world should notice that there's something very different about you. But this can happen only when you allow the Spirit to completely fill you. Just like one sip of wine would have no impact on a person's behavior, a sip of the Spirit here or there won't either. You must be filled.

Luke 4:1-2 puts it like this: "Jesus, full of the Holy Spirit, returned from the Jordan and was led around by the Spirit in the wilderness for forty days, being tempted by the devil. And He ate nothing during those days, and when they had ended, He became hungry." The word referring to Jesus being "full" of the Holy Spirit indicates He was "overwhelmed" by His presence. He was heavily influenced by the Spirit to the degree that He even allowed the Spirit to lead Him into the wilderness to face the devil.

Whenever you're full of something, that something controls you. Maybe you're full of sorrow, a condition Jesus attributed to His disciples in John 16:6. They were sad because He said He was leaving them, and that sadness was ruling their emotions and actions. Or perhaps you're full of rage just as Luke tells us people in Jesus' own hometown of Nazareth were when anger at His teaching had consumed them so much that they literally wanted to throw Him off the edge of a cliff (Luke 4:28-29).

In other words, to be "full" of something means releasing control to that something or to someone. Have you ever seen someone so full of anger that they seemed to be out of their mind? As a result, they didn't consider the consequences of their behavior. They did things they may have later regretted.

The world witnessed this kind of anger live on its TV screens (or in later reports) when during the film industry's 2022 Academy Awards ceremony, actor Will Smith charged comedian Chris Rock and then slapped him when one of the jokes Chris told had, in Smith's mind, insulted his wife, Jada. Anger filled Smith so much that it dominated his behavior, turning what should have been an evening of delight into an evening of destruction and national trauma.

Our emotions can overwhelm us as much as the effects of alcohol can. Or, often, the two combine to form a lethal dose of both, impacting decision-making in a debilitating way. Too much Hennessey or Jack Daniels can send a soul into a frenzy. But God wants to influence you in ways that will bring about good, not destruction. That's why He made His Spirit available to you—so you can be filled with the Spirit to such a degree that the Spirit directs your paths.

BEING FILLED IS NEVER MERELY AN OPTION

If you're going to be able to confront this evil world in such a way as to bring about good, you need to be influenced by God. His Spirit within you is what will enable you to maximize the time you're given in order to combat the evil of the culture. And the Holy Spirit provides what you need even in ways you didn't know you needed it.

In its original language, the Bible's term for "be filled" when talking about the Holy Spirit is a passive, present plural imperative. That means it's a command, not a suggestion. God isn't asking you to consider being filled. Nor is He recommending that you be filled. Paul, under the guidance of the Spirit in writing this passage in Ephesians, is *commanding* that you be filled. If you're going to gain access to the will of God so you can leverage your life in this land, you must be filled. It's not an option.

Now, you can reject the command to be filled, but if you choose to reject it, you'll remain asleep. You'll stay in a state of mind that makes you unable to even discern God's leading let alone tap into His power. This is why Paul writes that we are to be filled.

Yet the command Paul gives is also, interestingly, a passive term. It refers to something you allow to be done, not something you do yourself. For example, if I were to say, "I went to the store," that would be an active term. It would mean I physically went to the store. But if I were to say, "You took me to the store," then that is passive. I still made it to the store, but this time someone else took me there. I didn't take myself there.

To be filled with the Holy Spirit is a passive command. In other words, you do not fill yourself; the Holy Spirit fills you. So when Paul urges you and me to be filled, he is actually urging us to not block the Holy Spirit from filling us. He's urging us to allow the Spirit to do what only the Spirit can do in us. We must stop resisting the work of the Holy Spirit, because it is in releasing Him to work within us that we discover the power He has to supply.

Now, the term is also plural, not singular. If we were to put it in Texas lingo, it would be, "Ya'll, be filled." The Holy Spirit has come to fill each of us as the collective body of Jesus Christ. When Paul wrote to the church at Ephesus, he wrote to the whole church. He wasn't singling out any one person. He urged all of the saints there to wake up to the indwelling Spirit within them.

Just like you would expect every car to have fuel—gas or electricity—God expects every Christian to be full of the Spirit. Cars are made to run on fuel. A car without fuel is a useless car. Likewise, a Christian without the filling of the Spirit is a useless Christian. It's unacceptable for a believer to say, "Other people are filled by the Spirit, but I can't seem to be. I don't know how to be like them."

Again, being filled with the Spirit is not something you do; it's something you allow to be done to you. You have as much access to the Holy Spirit's filling as I do. The more believers in a church who constantly operate with the filling of the Spirit, the stronger that church will be. The fewer operating with the Spirit's filling, the weaker that church will be.

We all have equal access to the Spirit. What's more, as we see with

Paul's using the present tense of the term *fill*, we are to allow this filling to be an ongoing part of every moment. It's not something you do once and are done with it. Just like you wouldn't fill up your car with gas or charge it with electricity once and be done with it. You can't live on yesterday's filling of the Holy Spirit. What you got yesterday was meant for yesterday. The Holy Spirit is to fill you each and every day.

You may know Christians who like to talk about what God did for them yesterday, or even a few months or years ago. Sometimes even decades ago. It's almost as if God hasn't done anything for them lately. When testimonies of God's work in someone's life speak only of the past, you have to wonder if that person has fallen back asleep in their spiritual walk.

The Holy Spirit is a present participant in life's realities. Just like a car needs more fuel to keep going—or a person needs more alcohol to once more be drunk again—the filling of the Holy Spirit doesn't happen just once. It's an ongoing filling you allow to happen to you on a regular basis.

Most of us probably know what it's like to walk away from a church service or a spiritual event and feel full of the Holy Spirit. Somehow, our being together with others focused on God allows the Spirit to fill those who are open to Him even more. The atmosphere in these situations is often thick with the presence of God.

But then we also probably know what it's like to reach the parking lot after one of these services or events only to feel that the presence of the Spirit is dissipating. As we get into our car and hear the noises all around us, or strike up a conversation with our spouse, or turn on the radio to listen to the news, or even slip into traffic, we can literally feel it eroding and escaping. We no longer feel as spiritual as we did just minutes before inside the building's doors. While we said "Amen" and "Hallelujah" in the service, those words are nowhere near our lips now. Frustration even creeps in—as well as disappointment.

Like when a car leaves a gas station, the fuel has begun to burn away. Unfortunately, far too many people rely on the filling to take place at a church service or somewhere else external they can plug into. But if that isn't happening 24/7, you won't be in much of a good spot when it comes to living out your life. That kind of filling, the kind that's reliant on those around you to serve as a catalyst, doesn't last. It's up to you to discover how to allow an atmosphere of Holy Spirit filling to dominate your daily life. That's a decision you have to make, and those are actions you have to take in order to promote it.

TAKE STEPS TO BEING FILLED

You can't be full of the Spirit if you're full of yourself or sin. You can't be full of the Spirit if you're full of the latest binge TV show or your local sports team's ups and downs. You can't be full of the Spirit if you choose to give your predominant focus to something other than the Spirit's work in your life. The Holy Spirit will fill you only to the degree you make space for Him to do so.

Making space involves a key concept—surrendering to Jesus Christ. Until you surrender to Him, until you yield your life to Him on a continual basis while emptying yourself of anything else, you will not be filled by the Spirit. That includes filling yourself with yourself. Whenever you choose yourself over Jesus, the Holy Spirit has no space.

How to open ourselves to the Spirit's filling by surrendering to Jesus is given to us in chapter 5, verses 18 through 21 of Paul's letter to the church at Ephesus. You have a participatory role in the work of God in your life.

> Be filled with the Spirit, speaking to one another in psalms and hymns and spiritual songs, singing and making melody with your heart to the Lord; always giving thanks for all things in the name of our Lord Jesus Christ to God, even the Father; and be subject to one another in the fear of Christ.

In this passage, Paul lists a number of actions we can take to facilitate being filled. But to sum it up, we must consistently minister to

God as well as consistently minister to others from a good heart. Paul makes a point of saying we are to speak "to one another" but also "to the Lord." He also emphasizes gratitude as an atmosphere-creator for allowing the Spirit to fill us. Paul stated a very similar approach to the believers in Colossae when he wrote,

> Let the word of Christ richly dwell within you, with all wisdom teaching and admonishing one another with psalms and hymns and spiritual songs, singing with thankfulness in your hearts to God. Whatever you do in word or deed, do all in the name of the Lord Jesus, giving thanks through Him to God the Father (Colossians 3:16-17).

Whenever we prioritize God's Word through a grateful, surrendered heart in order to minister to God and to others, we've created the atmosphere for Spirit-filling. What Paul emphasizes in both of these passages is a lifestyle, not an event.

For too many of us, worship, gratitude, and even ministry are things we do, not a lifestyle we live. We're grateful in November when Thanksgiving reminds us to be. Or we worship on Sunday because the church doors have opened. Or we minister when the church sets up a food drive or special outreach Saturday event but at no other time or in no other place.

But Paul says none of that will do when it comes to being filled by the Spirit. Only when we live a life of ministry—singing songs to God and to others, reading His Word, surrendering to the Word of Christ, and talking about Him to others all the time—have we positioned ourselves for the filling of the Spirit.

Let's go back to our comparison between the wine of alcohol and the wine of the Spirit. I'm sure you're familiar with the phrase *social drinker.* That's someone who drinks at social events just to fit in. They don't plan to get drunk. In fact, a lot of social drinkers don't want to get drunk because they don't like the idea of losing control of their mental faculties. They're just trying to socialize with a sip here or there.

This is all too true when it comes to Christianity as well. We have "social Christians." Again using the concept of sipping, these individuals sip the Spirit in order to look the part and fit in. They sip a prayer here or there. But they don't want anything to do with being filled to the full by the Spirit of God. They want to keep their own control.

But sipping the Spirit will never give you access to the full power of the Spirit. Last I checked, there's only one way to get drunk. You have to drink. You don't get drunk by looking at wine. You don't get drunk by thinking about wine. You don't get drunk by praising certain aspects of wine. Nor do you get drunk by reading about wine. You get drunk by drinking wine—and lots of it. All those other things may make you sound informed and educated, but they won't make you intoxicated.

Similarly, you'll never be drunk with the Holy Spirit by thinking about Him, talking about Him, reading about Him, or seeing somebody else filled with Him. You get drunk on the Spirit only by drinking from Him—and regularly. You must maintain ongoing contact with the Spirit while promoting an atmosphere conducive to His filling. This includes hanging out with other Spirit-filled believers so you can stay spiritually intoxicated by the Spirit together, just as the believers of the early church did (Acts 4:31).

If you want this filling but you don't know where to start, Luke 11:13 gives you a good idea: "If you then, being evil, know how to give good gifts to your children, how much more will your heavenly Father give the Holy Spirit to those who ask Him?" Start by asking. Start by letting God know you want to be filled. Start by reminding Him as often as you can that you want to experience the fullness of the Spirit in your life. Then do what Paul mentioned doing to both the church at Ephesus and the church at Colossae—start ministering to God and to others every chance you get.

When you combine your prayers asking God to release the fullness of the Spirit in you with your active participation in advancing His kingdom agenda on earth through ministering to Him and to others, you will discover a whole new experience of God. The Holy Spirit will become more real to you than He has ever been.

And as a result, you will be transformed. In fact, your transformation will be so noticeable that even those around you will make comments about the change and ask what's happened. You will become a witness to the world, an alarm of your own doing that will contribute to the waking of those who have fallen back to sleep.

7

THE FRUIT

This chapter is about the Holy Spirit as the Fruit, but first let's talk about crabs.

One of the things I loved to do when I was growing up in Baltimore was eating steamed crabs. And I still love to eat them anytime I return there to speak or to visit family. Maryland is known for having some of the best crabs in the country, with many millions of them harvested out of Chesapeake Bay. People throw crab parties. Or you can often find a crab feast hosted somewhere. Crabs have become the known delicacy of the state. In fact, people come from all around the country to eat these steamed, well-seasoned crustaceans.

Whenever my dad could afford it, he brought crabs home on Friday night—something to look forward to all week long. My brothers, sister, and my parents and I would indulge ourselves on the delicious treat all evening long. It became a family tradition—again, one I repeat on most visits up that way.

Now, if you've ever seen live crabs being steamed (yes, they're best when cooked alive), you've probably noticed this about the process. When the water heats up, they try to escape. They want to leave the boil.

But inevitably, as one crab tries to climb out of the pot, another crab will grab it and pull it back down because it wants out of the heat of the pot too. Or it will try to step on the first crab in order to get to the top.

That cycle continues as crab after crab tries to climb out, only to prevent them all from climbing out. Their claws merely destroy and devour one another in the same shared place of destruction.

Paul was concerned about this crab-like mentality in the church at Galatia. He was concerned about Christians devouring one another. And we read about his concerns in Galatians 5:13-15:

> You were called to freedom, brethren; only do not turn your freedom into an opportunity for the flesh, but through love serve one another. For the whole Law is fulfilled in one word, in the statement, "You shall love your neighbor as yourself." But if you bite and devour one another, take care that you are not consumed by one another.

Paul voiced his concern that the Christians were devouring and destroying one another rather than enabling, serving, helping, building up, and loving one another. Instead of doing what God had created them to do, they were pulling others down like live crabs in a pot of boiling water. Paul referred to this with harsh words—*bite* and *devour*.

I would be curious to know what Paul might say if he spent just a few moments on Twitter or other social media platforms and caught a glimpse of what Christians post. Or if he visited a church or small group and heard the whispers behind the scenes. The problems so prevalent all around us today—whether cultural, racial, political, or any other—have induced an atmosphere of vitriolic hate.

But while that reality may be true for the world as a general rule, it ought not to be normative among the people of God. God doesn't want us clamoring, clawing, and yanking one another down in our desperation to lift ourselves up. Rather, He wants us all out of the pot. He wants us all to experience biblical freedom, released from illegitimate bondage so we can maximize our spiritual calling and potential.

THE FRUIT OF THE SPIRIT

This name, the Fruit, representing the person and work of the Holy Spirit, is key to helping each of us unlock our greatest potential for Christ. The Spirit's fruit is His ability to assist believers in bearing *their* fruit.

Paul talks about the Spirit as a fruit-bearing tree allowing believers to maximize their spiritual productivity and Christlike character. After calling out the Christians in Galatia, he then points them to how they ought to be treating one another. He introduces them to the fruit of the Spirit, and we uncover this fruit in Galatians 5:22-26:

> The fruit of the Spirit is love, joy, peace, patience, kindness, goodness, faithfulness, gentleness, self-control; against such things there is no law. Now those who belong to Christ Jesus have crucified the flesh with its passions and desires. If we live by the Spirit, let us also walk by the Spirit. Let us not become boastful, challenging one another, envying one another.

Paul emphasizes how we are to relate to one another—by reflecting the Holy Spirit's person and work within us. Rather than being destructive toward one another, we are to be healing agents for good. Rather than bickering, blaming, and backstabbing in the body of Christ, we are to reflect the fruit of the Spirit. Only the Spirit can address and rectify the depth of division that has crept into Christian circles today.

The antidote to the calamity and chaos among us, particularly among believers, is the Spirit. We are to walk according to the Spirit, not according to our flesh. Paul tells us how to do that if we take a moment to back up in this passage and read verses 16-18:

> I say, walk by the Spirit, and you will not carry out the desire of the flesh. For the flesh sets its desire against the Spirit, and the Spirit against the flesh; for these are in

opposition to one another, so that you may not do the
things that you please. But if you are led by the Spirit, you
are not under the Law.

Paul calls to our attention a civil war taking place between the flesh
and the Spirit within us. The flesh is that desire in you to please yourself independently of God. In other words, you want to please yourself
in a way that goes outside God's prescribed means. Yet the Spirit is the
presence of Christ within each of us that stirs a desire to please God
even more than we aim to please ourselves.

Paul explains that the difference here is driven by desire. The civil
war waging within has to do with a craving to be satisfied, which then
tries to snuff out the desire to please God. The Spirit wants to please
God; the flesh wants to please ourselves. These two lead to an inner
clash that every believer has to deal with.

SIN REMAINS

Before you were saved, you had only the flesh to deal with. You
had a sin nature, and it acted like a factory to produce sin time and
time again. Just like a car factory produces cars, your sin nature produced sinful thoughts, desires, and actions. Yet when you accepted
Jesus Christ into your life, God shut down the sin factory. The factory
was closed because God gave you a new nature. As we see in 2 Corinthians 5:17, "If anyone is in Christ, he is a new creature; the old things
passed away; behold, new things have come."

The new creature is the Spirit within. But an issue that often con-
fuses believers is this: If the sin factory has been closed and replaced
by a new creation, the Spirit, then why do we still have to battle with
our flesh at all?

The reason is because the factory has already produced the "cars,"
and they're already out "on the road." When an automobile factory
shuts down, the cars it produced don't stop being out on the highway.

They're still there. Similarly, the sin nature within us produced sinful thoughts, worldviews, goals, and actions, and those produce ripple effects and habitual cycles that go on in time in our souls and bodies.

One of the reasons we have to die before we go to heaven or God has to change us in the rapture, is because the body of this world has become contaminated by the cars on the road that were produced by the sin factory we all possessed at birth. It has infiltrated our beings and our world. Now, it's not only our own sinfulness we must contend with but also the sins of everyone else. We've all contributed to an atmosphere of sin that replicates in thoughts, words, and actions. When we go to heaven, we will be given a brand-new body inhabited by a perfectly transformed soul so that we can function in an atmosphere of purity. But in the meantime, as we live among unredeemed humanity, we continue to face the lure and trappings of sin.

In other words, sin still operates not just in the world but within every believer. Paul refers to our bodies as the body of sin. This is why we have the struggles we do. In fact, one of the ways you know you're spiritual is that you're in a fight against temptation. You can also tell you're growing spiritually because the Spirit wars against the flesh, and the flesh wars against the Spirit. Temptation is the appeal to the desire of sin embedded in the flesh. This always leads to that desire to be satisfied independently of God.

The solution to yielding to temptation lies with the Spirit. As Paul mentioned in Galatians 5:16, "But I say, walk by the Spirit, and you will not carry out the desire of the flesh."

You don't overcome the flesh by fixing the flesh. The flesh is unfixable. You can't keep your flesh from being fleshy; it's already been invaded by sin. This shows up at a very young age. My oldest great-granddaughter illustrated this so well recently. Her name is Ellie, and like other kids do, she loves to sneak food from the kitchen. On this day, and even though she'd been corrected for this disobedience a number of times, she sneaked some ice cream and hid it under her bed. She planned to eat it as soon as her parents weren't anywhere nearby, hopefully before it melted!

The problem is that her little brother found the ice cream, and instead of covering for her and making a deal to share the ice cream, he told on her.

I'm sure you've seen similar things happen with your kids or kids you know—or maybe you did sneaky things like that when you were a kid. That's because children, though so young, know how to sin. It's built into their very nature. It's built into their flesh. We never have to teach a child how to lie, steal, or disobey. We don't have to instruct them on what to do wrong.

Rather, we have to teach children what to do right. We have to teach them to share, to be kind, and to be considerate. We have to teach children gratitude, patience, and compassion. And that's because everyone's sin natures dominates their life until they learn to walk in the Spirit.

People spend an inordinate amount of money on counseling and all kinds of therapies to try to make the flesh less fleshy. And while I believe counseling and therapy are important—and I've counseled thousands of people in my role as a pastor—the bottom line is always about whether the Spirit is allowed to dominate over the flesh. Without this understanding, we have to settle for flesh management instead of spiritual transformation.

Any bodybuilder knows our bodies are made up of both fat and muscle. Oftentimes, if you're trying to lose fat, you're also trying to build muscle. But we can't turn fat into muscle. Fat is fat. Muscle is muscle. We have to lose the fat and build the muscle, but we can never change the fat into muscle because they're two distinct realities in our physical frames.

Similarly, the flesh and the Spirit are distinct. You are born with the flesh, but you won't get rid of it by trying to turn it into the Spirit. You can't self-regulate your flesh into obedience. You can only reduce the flesh's influence while simultaneously strengthening the Spirit's influence in your life. You reduce the power of the flesh as you grow in walking in the Spirit.

Paul put it like this in Galatians 3:1-5:

> You foolish Galatians, who has bewitched you, before whose eyes Jesus Christ was publicly portrayed as cruci-fied? This is the only thing I want to find out from you: did you receive the Spirit by the works of the Law, or by hear-ing with faith? Are you so foolish? Having begun by the Spirit, are you now being perfected by the flesh? Did you suffer so many things in vain—if indeed it was in vain? So then, does He who provides you with the Spirit and works miracles among you, do it by the works of the Law, or by hearing with faith?

Paul let the Galatians know they had been duped by flesh-management programs, sermons, and more. They'd bought into the lie that far too many preachers promote today—that their job is to fix their flesh. But the goal of the Christian life is never to fix the flesh. The goal of the Holy Spirit is to override the flesh. You can't change the flesh from being what it is. You can only experience true transforma-tion by allowing the person and work of the Spirit to be made mani-fest in your life. When you walk with the Spirit, Paul says in Galatians 5:16, you will not carry out the flesh's desires.

Now, keep in mind that Paul doesn't say you will no longer have the desires of the flesh. He doesn't say your flesh will stop wanting to sin or craving that which it lusts after. What Paul does say is that you will no longer carry out the flesh's desires. His very statement lets us know that the desires may still be there; you just won't carry them out.

Paul speaks from experience when he writes to the church at Gala-tia. In the book of Romans, he shares his personal struggle with his flesh. If you read through chapter 7, you'll see him wrestling with it. He doesn't tell us what the specific fleshy thing he's wrestling with is, but he does let us know it's difficult to overcome. In fact, he even gets to the point of deep despair. In Romans 7:24 he cries out, "Wretched man that I am! Who will set me free from the body of this death?"

Paul desperately longed to break free. His flesh continued to prod him to do that which he did not want to do. He wrestled with it until he came to the conclusion he revealed to us in Romans 8:1-4:

> There is now no condemnation for those who are in Christ Jesus. For the law of the Spirit of life in Christ Jesus has set you free from the law of sin and of death. For what the Law could not do, weak as it was through the flesh, God did: sending His own Son in the likeness of sinful flesh and as an offering for sin, He condemned sin in the flesh, so that the requirement of the Law might be fulfilled in us, who do not walk according to the flesh but according to the Spirit.

If you want to overcome the flesh, you do it by learning to walk according to the Spirit. Paul had to come to this realization in his own life, as we all do. It's not about getting to the point where you never feel or experience temptation or fleshly desires. It's not about perfecting yourself. It's about learning how to no longer yield to those desires so the flesh doesn't dominate your choices.

Yielding is entirely different from having. The flesh will always rear its ugly head. But the way you overcome its influence on your life is not through trying to obey every law given to mankind but through recognizing that it's only according to the law of the Spirit and your walk with the Spirit that He will produce His work in you to set you free from the control of the flesh.

THE SOLUTION: LEARN TO WALK IN THE SPIRIT

The law of gravity is a non negotiable law. It's just the way our world functions. What goes up must come down. It's a physical law. We can fly on an airplane and not come crashing down due to the law of gravity. Why? Because another law supersedes the law of gravity—the law of aerodynamics. This law says when you move at a certain speed given the right amount of thrust, you don't cancel out gravity, but you do override it. Gravity still exists doing what gravity always does. But the thrust of the plane's engine coupled with its speed lifts the plane out of the stranglehold of gravity. Gravity no longer has to make the final decision when it comes to our flying in a plane.

The Spirit acts in much the same way this law of aerodynamics acts toward the law of gravity. While there's a law of sin that wages war in the members of our bodies, the law of the Spirit can override the law of sin, enabling us to rise above it. The solution to every relational issue you face is found in learning to walk in the Spirit. The solution to every internal conflict or lust you face is found in learning to walk in the Spirit. The solution to every addiction or bad habit you face is found in learning to walk in the Spirit. In fact, the solution to any sin issue you face is found in this same process of learning to walk in the Spirit.

No matter how strong sin's pull is on your flesh and desires, it will not have the final say when the law of the Spirit is let loose in your life. The person and work of the Spirit produces the fruit of the Spirit in you, which is then expanded and expressed through your life. Just as gravity will do everything in its power to try to keep a plane from taking off, sin will also seek to keep you stuck in its grip. But that's why you must fully unleash the Spirit's power so you can benefit from His overriding strength.

Now, your flesh won't like your bringing the Spirit to bear on every decision or choice you make. It wants you to think only about yourself. But when you stop trying to defeat the flesh or beat it into submission and just realize the flesh will always be the flesh, you can tap into that which is a greater law. The law of love as manifested in the law of the Spirit thus overrides the flesh's control over you so the Spirit can produce His fruit in your life.

You unleash this law of love in your life when you walk by the Spirit. Walking is a great analogy, because it gives us three areas to consider for how we are to live—destination, dependency, and dedication:

1. Destination

First, when you walk, there is always a destination in mind. You're going somewhere. Rarely does anyone walk aimlessly unless something is wrong with that person's mind. Similarly, when you walk, you move toward that destination. You don't just think about it. Thus, walking in the Spirit is not passive. It doesn't involve your sitting down and waiting for a jolt from heaven. You're doing the walking while the Spirit is doing the empowering.

Walking in the Spirit means to actively pursue the destination of spiritual maturity and kingdom impact. You're walking toward the will of God for your life. And to walk in the will of God, which is the realm of the Spirit, you must make a conscious decision to identify God's will and make your way toward it. Now, identifying God's will is its own thing, but it can be done based on God's Word and the illumination you receive from the Spirit. Inviting the Spirit into the activity of the atmosphere of personal growth and calling will flip on the switch in your spirit to discern the will of God.

2. Dependency

Second, when it comes to walking, there's a dependency. You put one foot in front of the other, placing all of your weight on one leg until you can put it on the other. You're dependent on your legs to get you where you need to go. Similarly, when you choose to walk in the Spirit, you're surrendering dependency on yourself and choosing instead to depend on God. You're no longer counting on your flesh to get you where you need to be. You're counting on God to do that. This dependency is expressed through prayer.

3. Dedication

Third, walking always includes dedication. It's never done half-heartedly if you plan to get anywhere. You don't take one step forward and then two steps back, or just one step and then stop. That's not considered walking. Walking means you're dedicated to moving consistently toward a destination. You are committed.

If you decide to go for a walk for some exercise starting from home, and you typically like to take a certain two-mile loop, you can't just opt out at the beginning of the second mile. You can't just sit down on the path or the sidewalk and declare that's as far as you're going to walk for the day. You'll need to be dedicated enough to finish it.

Walking with the Spirit requires dedication as well. It requires movements that demonstrate you believe what the Holy Spirit is telling you about God's will. God wants to see your faith, not just hear about your faith. He wants to see the steps you're taking as you seek to uncover and maximize His will in your life. These steps of faith validate your faith and activate the Spirit's work in your life.

After all, faith is not a feeling. You can be full of faith and have no feelings about it. Or you can have plenty of feelings but not have faith. Faith is faith when it's demonstrated by the movements you take, not just by what you say or feel.

LEAN ON THE SPIRIT AS YOU LEARN

Walking by the Spirit is an action, and it's akin to walking by faith. You may not do it perfectly at first. But that's okay. Sometimes you have to work your muscles before you can set out on longer walks. Or you have to learn to walk altogether. Whatever your case, the Holy Spirit is there to help you.

I'm sure you've seen a baby reach the stage of trying to walk. There's a lot of falling. He might take only one step before going down. Or she might take two steps before dropping to the floor. Regardless, you can be sure the baby's parents or grandparents are clapping and cheering the baby onward. Do you think they would ever scold that baby for only managing one step or two? Or would they ever be disappointed when the baby made it only a little ways before falling? No, I don't think so either. They usually rush over to help the baby get back up and try again.

The Holy Spirit doesn't laugh at us for trying to walk by faith, then failing. He doesn't hold out a standard that says we must walk ten miles wearing our body weight in strap-on weights. The Holy Spirit is there to help us learn how to walk spiritually, every step of the way. Eventually, just like for babies, walking in faith will become second nature. It will become a lifestyle. But until that time comes, don't be shy to lean on the Spirit to help you as you build and develop your spiritual muscles. Look to the Spirit, and He will guide you as you grow. Romans 8:5-6 is a great reminder on how this works:

> Those who are according to the flesh set their minds on the things of the flesh, but those who are according to the Spirit, the things of the Spirit. For the mind set on the flesh is death, but the mind set on the Spirit is life and peace.

Essentially, this passage tells us that if we have a walking problem, it's because we have a problem of our minds. We aren't thinking right. We aren't thinking spiritually. When you and I choose to think about our flesh using human wisdom, we cease to walk in the Spirit. We forfeit the life and peace that come from walking with Him. Walking with another person is a relational activity, and walking in the Spirit is no different. Give the Spirit your attention as you walk with Him. That's when you'll discover the power and presence of His love.

Galatians 5:18 shows us what happens when we walk by the Spirit's leading in our lives: "If you are led by the Spirit, you are not under the Law." Just as in the overcoming of the law of gravity through the law of aerodynamics, being led by the Spirit frees you from the chains of the law of sin. Have you ever seen a dog owner using a leash? They manage its distance and movement because they don't want their dog to run off. They do it in order to protect their pet.

But other dogs are trained to stay near their owners without a leash.

Their relationship is so strong that they don't need a restraint to keep them from running away. When you and I develop a close relationship with the Holy Spirit, we are free from the power of law over us. The law does not need to hold us hostage, because we have chosen to obey the law of love, God's greatest commandments—to love Him and to love others.

PRODUCING GOOD FRUIT

The deeds of our flesh are always self-centered. Fruit that eats itself is rotten. But the fruit of the Spirit is always beneficial to others, and you'll know how well you're walking with the Spirit by your deeds. Jesus said a similar thing in John 13:35: "By this all men will know that you are My disciples, if you have love for one another." The fruit will reveal where your heart lies.

Again, Paul put it like this in the same letter to the church at Galatia we've been exploring in this chapter:

> The fruit of the Spirit is love, joy, peace, patience, kindness, goodness, faithfulness, gentleness, self-control; against such things there is no law. Now those who belong to Christ Jesus have crucified the flesh with its passions and desires. If we live by the Spirit, let us also walk by the Spirit (Galatians 5:22-25).

There is no law against that kind of fruit. What's more, that fruit will produce more fruit after its own kind. When you walk according to the person and work of the Spirit within, not only will you override sin's pull on you but simultaneously produce healthy, life-giving fruit that will bring God glory, others good, and you joy. All of this is free to you if you will just choose to walk with the Spirit.

Make the choice to get up and start moving toward the destination of God's will for your life based on His Word. Depend on the Spirit as you do. And stay determined and committed to keep going no matter what may happen along the way. When you do that, you'll be amazed at how great the plan God has for you and how perfect is the destiny He's chosen for you to fulfill.

8

THE INTERCESSOR

Even if only through films or TV dramas, we all know the pain associated with childbirth is real. Yet the groans of a woman in labor, which sound like bad news, signal a good situation. Childbirth hurts, yes, but it's because someone new is about to be born.

Now, I get it. The fact that someone new is being birthed doesn't negate the pain of the process. But neither is the pain of the process limited to pain. The pain exists to produce a greater joy and reality.

This reality for all of us is that life hurts. Its difficulties, traumas, and hidden troubles come to us—and often at the most inopportune times. We'd all love a life with no pain, anguish, or sorrow, but if you've lived long enough to know, you know that isn't an option. Again, life hurts. And as I've become all too familiar with recently, at times circumstances and loss both affect you and infect you to such a degree that all you can do is groan.

Have you ever been there? Do you know what it's like to run out of words to explain what you're going through? Have you experienced those seasons when you don't even have the strength to pray anymore? At one point or another, most of us have. Which is why God has given us this next name of the Holy Spirit. In Romans 8, we pick up looking at Paul's struggle between the flesh and the spirit, and as we do, we come across a most powerful and needed character attribute and role of the Holy Spirit. He is the Intercessor.

An intercessor appeals to someone on behalf of a situation or another person. They are a go-between, like lawyers who plead their clients' cases before a judge or jury. They intercede in situations that are due to troubles or difficulties. And Romans 8 tells us we have an intercessor when life causes us to groan. We have a representative when we face suffering. In short, we have hope.

THE INTERCESSOR BRINGS HOPE

Suffering is the pain of negative circumstances or even unmet expectations. When this pain hits you so hard that it overwhelms you, you need someone else to lend a helping hand. Paul was intimately familiar with this pain, and he wrote to us about it in Romans 8:22-25:

> We know that the whole creation groans and suffers the pains of childbirth together until now. And not only this, but also we ourselves, having the first fruits of the Spirit, even we ourselves groan within ourselves, waiting eagerly for our adoption as sons, the redemption of our body. For in hope we have been saved, but hope that is seen is not hope; for who hopes for what he already sees? But if we hope for what we do not see, with perseverance we wait eagerly for it.

Paul begins by telling us that suffering is literally part of the created order. He relates the groaning of childbirth to the groaning of earth itself through creation. This gives us a theological and spiritual way to understand earthquakes, tsunamis, hurricanes, tornadoes, and other natural disasters that seem to come out of nowhere, including a pandemic caused by a virus. When these things erupt, they're not benign events. They wreak havoc on the lives of those impacted by them, but they also wreak havoc on the natural world order.

These are the groanings of the globe. They let us know creation itself is in pain. To live in this world is to live in a world that groans.

But Paul reflects on this by comparing it to our own pain. He says the groaning we see in creation is like a woman groaning as she gives birth. These groans only come louder and grow closer together the nearer the baby is to being born. More frequent groaning and greater volume often indicates the baby is about to arrive. Scripture tells us we can recognize the signs of the end times in a similar way when God is about to give birth to a new dispensation. Jesus referred to earthquakes and other natural occurrences as an indicator prior to the great persecution of Christians on earth. We read this in Luke 21:7 and verses 10-11:

> They questioned Him, saying, "Teacher, when therefore will these things happen? And what will be the sign when these things are about to take place?"…Then He continued by saying to them, "Nation will rise against nation and kingdom against kingdom, and there will be great earthquakes, and in various places plagues and famines; and there will be terrors and great signs from heaven."

If and when we view suffering only for suffering's sake and neglect to view it through a theological lens, we miss out on the spiritual meanings behind it. If you see only the pain, you'll miss out on the purpose. You must cooperate with the purpose for the purpose to produce fruit. But when we can't cooperate due to a lack of strength or for any other reason, God has provided an intercessor for us. When we can only groan at our own or a loved one's sickness or when confronted with personal loss, the Holy Spirit is our source of strength.

If you have ever groaned at disappointments with people—even with yourself—or with your career or for dreams that wound up dashed, causing you to ache within, you know how important this name of the Holy Spirit truly is. If you have a soul ache causing all hope within you to collapse in on itself like an internal tornado ripping at the very core of your being, this name is for you. Because if you're a believer, you have Someone who loves you enough and cares about you enough to intervene on your behalf.

But for the Holy Spirit as the Intercessor to intervene on your behalf, you need to look to Him to do so.

Suffering is simply a reminder to each of us that this life is not all there is. This world is not all that exists. We are never to make more out of it than we ought to, even though that's so easy to do. So when you're groaning within the depths of your soul like a woman groans for her deliverance in childbirth, it's time to shift your focus. Pain is designed to produce a spiritual shift, and if and when you don't make it, you'll be left to deal with the loss alone.

This is why God allows reminders that will force us toward a spiritual perspective to enter into our existence. He will use loved ones to do that at times. He will use our emotions to do that at times. And He will use our bodies to do that at times. He allows aches, pains, and bruises to produce a new perspective.

Yet whenever you or I fail to allow the groanings to recalibrate our thinking, we also fail to experience the benefit of the Intercessor. Romans 8:6 explains the difference between experiencing the Spirit and not experiencing Him: "For the mind set on the flesh is death, but the mind set on the Spirit is life and peace."

The mind set on the flesh—which looks at life only through a human lens—does not experience life and peace. It functions from the viewpoint of a funeral home. When our minds focus on the human limitations of this life, we live in the realm of death. We never get to know God's reality on earth because we're confined by our own. The end result of all flesh is death. Whether that's the death of dreams, hopes, desires, or even our physical realities, this world offers only what remains in this world.

Yet the mind set on the Spirit is life and peace. It is akin to walking out of a funeral home on a bright, sunny day and hearing the birds chirp, feeling the nice breeze blow by you, and seeing the flowers bloom, knowing that the spiritual realm goes beyond the walls of our five senses. If you live your life void of God and His perspective, you live where an eternal view is out of your reach. Life and peace are found only when you understand the spiritual nature of the soul you've been blessed to embody in human form.

But it's easy to forget the spiritual when the pain of the physical dominates our psyche, and that is why Paul reminds us of the Spirit's key role. He writes,

> The Spirit also helps our weakness; for we do not know how
> to pray as we should, but the Spirit Himself intercedes for
> us with groanings too deep for words (Romans 8:26).

When the pain is so deep that you can't even get the words out, or all you can do is cry because the hurt is like a hurricane within, the Holy Spirit is there to help you. The Spirit helps the most when you're at your lowest, in your weaknesses. Paul tells us that's when He intercedes on our behalf with His own groanings too deep for words. He goes to God on our behalf to seek our relief and the way out of the depths of pain that engulf us.

PAUL'S TRANSPARENCY

Paul didn't write this from a mere intellectual perspective. He knew pain personally. He referred to a specific season of difficulty as a great ordeal of affliction. He said things got so bad that he ultimately gave up. Arguably the most spiritual man in the New Testament got to a point where the best he could look forward to in his life was death. Don't take my word for it. Listen to Paul himself:

> We do not want you to be unaware, brethren, of our afflic-
> tion which came to us in Asia, that we were burdened

> excessively, beyond our strength, so that we despaired even of life; indeed, we had the sentence of death within ourselves so that we would not trust in ourselves (2 Corinthians 1:8-9).

Paul's saying "sentence of death" was just another way to say he was emotionally suicidal. When death looks brighter than life, a person is operating from a suicidal standpoint. Thus, even spiritual people can get there. Even spiritual people can long for death more than life or wish to be set free from the confines of this world. They can become so weak that they no longer know how they're going to make it at all.

I hope Paul's transparency will help you have greater courage. I hope his despair lifts your spirit some, if only in that you know you are not alone. You aren't the only one who's reached the point of wanting to quit, give up, or throw in the towel. When life crashes in on you and you feel oppressed from every side, take comfort in realizing that others have also walked this path. Others have clung to the walls of the pit unsure if they should keep climbing or just let go.

The apostle Paul is one of them. So if he can hit rock bottom, anyone can. Spiritual people can, and do, hit rock bottom. We are human. And life does hurt.

But as we continue reading this passage in 2 Corinthians, Paul gives us insight into why God sometimes allows us to face more than we can bear on our own. He writes,

> Indeed, we had the sentence of death within ourselves so that we would not trust in ourselves, but in God who raises the dead; who delivered us from so great a peril of death, and will deliver us, He on whom we have set our hope (verses 9-10).

Paul was forced into a spiritual perspective when life got too hard to handle on his own. That's when he realized why God had allowed everything he'd gone through—so he would learn this valuable lesson: It's always better to hope in God than to trust in yourself.

This may seem like an easy lesson if you're just stating it. But to actually live in alignment with it as truth is a lot more difficult for all of us. When you understand this truth, it changes the decisions you make, and it also changes your emotions within those decisions. It changes your prayer life. It changes your testimony. It changes everything.

THE HOLY SPIRIT IS OUR GO-BETWEEN

I wish I could tell you that life won't collapse and the walls won't feel as if they're caving in. I wish I could say that will be true for you. But as I know from my own experience, life does collapse, and when it does, it crashes down hard. Sometimes all at once. I lost eight family members in the span of two years—my wife, my father, my sister, my niece, and four more. I wish I could tell you God will never give you more than you can bear. But I can't tell you that, because it's not in the Bible. It's not scriptural. It's not true.

But I can tell you that when the world crashes in on you, you have Someone who will show up as an intercessor when you need Him the most. The Holy Spirit will pray for you when you don't have the words to pray for yourself. He will take your inarticulate expressions of anguish and turn them into a powerful prayer to God because He knows God as part of the Holy Trinity.

He also knows what parts of your heart's prayer to take to God in order to connect with His will and desires for your life. He's like a great negotiator who knows how to bring both sides to the table for a win-win scenario. In Romans 8:27 we read, "He who searches the hearts knows what the mind of the Spirit is, because He intercedes for the saints according to the will of God." The Holy Spirit takes your greatest needs to the throne room of God, but He does so in a way that provides the best possible connection with God's will. He communicates with God according to what interests Him the most and in a way He comprehends the best. He creates a vocabulary that fits the environment that needs to hear what you have to say.

Every Sunday at our church, people perform sign language for the hearing impaired, individuals who need the words communicated to them in an entirely different way than verbally. While I could never preach in ASL myself, the interpreters translate what I say into a language those people in our pews understand as well as countless other hearing-impaired people worldwide watching on our streaming channel. They act as the in-between representatives between me and those who need the ministry of the Word.

The Holy Spirit is our in-between representative between heaven and earth. Whether bringing heavenly language to our ears and hearts or bringing earthly cries to God's throne, the Holy Spirit intercedes and communicates on our behalf. The Spirit, like Christ, knows God better than anyone else (1 Corinthians 2:10-16). The Holy Spirit and God are like those married couples who just have to look at each other to know what the other is thinking. No words need to be said. The relationship is so intimate that one look can equate to an entire paragraph or more.

When you're in a foreign country and don't know the language there, you need either an interpreter or an interpretation app on your phone. You need someone or something to be an intercessor between you and the people you're talking with in order for communication to take place. The Holy Spirit serves in this capacity for us since we don't know how to speak the language of heaven—and sometimes, even when we have difficulty expressing our deepest needs in the languages on earth. The Spirit can hear our spirit within when we don't have the words to express what we're feeling.

God isn't interested in empty words. He wants to hear what our heart is saying when we cry out to Him. Isaiah 29:13 emphasizes this truth for us: "Then the Lord said, 'Because this people draw near with their words and honor Me with their lip service, but they remove their hearts far from Me, and their reverence for Me consists of tradition learned by rote…'" God wants your heart to draw close to Him so He can hear the expressions of your spirit within. You do this through the Holy Spirit, who lives to intercede on your behalf.

Anytime you're trying to reach God in the midst of your pain, that pain may distort your thinking. You may not know what to ask for in accordance with God's will. This is because you're just trying to address the pain and remove it, fix it, or change it. But the prayers that are answered are those given in alignment with God's will. As 1 John 5:14-15 says, "This is the confidence which we have before Him, that, if we ask anything according to His will, He hears us. And if we know that He hears us in whatever we ask, we know that we have the requests which we have asked from Him."

If a prayer is in the will of God, it will be answered in relation to the request of the prayer. If it is not, it won't be. God guarantees only what He wills. Thus, the idea of prayer is to discern what God wills and then ask for that. But you and I don't always know how to discern what God wants. Or maybe we can't discern His timing.

Whatever the case may be, we need the Holy Spirit, who can know what our issue is yet know what God's will is. He can then seek to connect the two where they naturally merge. Or He can seek to influence our hearts to align more with God's will. The Holy Spirit will take our desires and clarify our requests so they align with God's will as much as possible. That's the best way to experience answered prayer when we don't know what to pray or how to pray at any given moment in time.

Let's take a moment for some honesty here. Isn't instant relief what we're really hoping for when we pray? We pray as though we're placing an order for relief with Amazon's same-day service. We don't want it delivered tomorrow; we want it delivered today. But we won't get the relief we need until we learn how to pray according to God's will. God has a specific will for your life and for mine. The Holy Spirit's role is to help us conform to God's will. This is often done through a doctrine called providence—the mysterious way God intercedes and interconnects things in order to unite them for His sovereign purpose.

An important distinction must be made between God's providence and His miracles. A miracle is when God transcends His laws He built into creation. Miracles are when He skips the natural law, or cancels it, in order to accomplish His aim. A lot of things we call miracles aren't really miracles. A miracle is when God operates outside the natural established law, which He set up in order to reach His goal.

But providence is different from that. Providence is when God works within His natural laws to stitch things together in order to weave them into the place of alignment with His will. It's the way He connects things in order to support His sovereignty.

Now, in order for you to see His providential work in your life, particularly in those times that seem to be full of pain, you must have a heart that's in love with Him. And to love God is to passionately pursue His glory. It's not just a feeling; it's a decision you make—to passionately pursue glorifying Him. It's in stating *Not my will but Your will be done.* Or saying *Not my kingdom but Your Kingdom come.* Loving God means living a life that is God-ward. You're always taking His view into consideration. When you do that, He works everything out for His plan for your life.

Romans 8:28 tells us this truth. You're probably familiar with this verse, but we often don't connect it to the two verses preceding it, which we've already been looking at in this chapter. Only when we read this entire passage in context do we understand what God is ultimately up to. What's more, only when we connect Romans 8:28 with the verse that follows it do we gain a better understanding into *why* God will work everything out for us.

Again, Romans 8:26-27 says,

> In the same way the Spirit also helps our weakness; for we do not know how to pray as we should, but the Spirit Himself intercedes for us with groanings too deep for words; and He who searches the hearts knows what the mind of the Spirit is, because He intercedes for the saints according to the will of God.

And then Romans 28-29 says,

We know that God causes all things to work together for good to those who love God, to those who are called according to His purpose. For those whom He foreknew, He also predestined to become conformed to the image of His Son, so that He would be the firstborn among many brethren.

TRANSFORMING AND CONFORMING

You can be assured that God is causing all things to work together for good when you love Him. It may be painful at the moment. You may not understand the pain in the midst of it. But if you're called according to His purposes, primarily that of becoming conformed to the image of His Son, Jesus Christ, God will work things out for good. The Holy Spirit seeks to do this by interceding on your behalf when you need Him to do that. The Holy Spirit aims to shape your heart God-ward all the while interceding to God for you in the areas of your greatest needs. This is the process of conforming to the image of Christ.

The Bible talks a lot about being transformed, and one of the ways God transforms us is by making us conformed. To transform something is to change it from the inside out. But to conform something is to mold it from the outside. Conforming is what you do with putty or clay. You can make a plate or bowl when you squeeze it, mash it, and shape it. God allows external circumstances in our lives in order to transform us internally. He also does this in order to conform us into the image of Christ. Conforming produces the transformation within.

If God is stretching you, pressing you, and allowing all manner of difficulty to happen to you—and you love Him—then be assured that He is seeking to conform you to Christ. He wants to develop something in you by shifting things outside of you in order to transform you. The Holy Spirit knows you better than you know yourself, and the Spirit also knows God. When you allow the Spirit to be your intercessor, you can count on His aligning you with God's will in the best possible way to connect with your desires or change them. You don't have to try to figure things out when you trust the Spirit as your intercessor. You just have to yield to His role in your heart.

That's why rather than making a list of everything you want or all the problems you fear up ahead, you should be spending your time thanking the Spirit. Thank Him for pleading your case before God so that all things can be rightly stitched together in time. Thank Him that even though you can't see it now, you don't know how it will work out, and you don't understand what is happening, you know the Spirit does, and you trust His hand in your life. Thank the Spirit that, due to His active role in you, you know God will work things out for good. When your mind focuses on what you have to be grateful for with regard to the Spirit and His work both in and through you, you will find the peace you long for.

God is always working. He is never still, even when He seems silent. You may not see what He's doing, but He has a plan, and He's bringing it all together for good for those who love Him and are called according to His purposes. Yes, when good comes into your life, it may feel like luck sometimes, or it may seem like some people get lucky. But there is no such thing as luck. There is only providence. You didn't just happen to wind up with the good things or good people in your life. God providentially arranged things so you were at the right place at the right time—if your heart sought Him and loves Him.

Now, if you don't love God, then I don't think this book will be much help to you. Nor will the Spirit be much help to you, even though He is present within every believer. Your heart has a choice. It's up to you how much or how little you love God. But just remember this: Every choice has a resultant consequence. If you choose to love God and walk in His ways, you will experience the Spirit's power of interceding on your behalf. But it starts with you. It starts with your heart. Your mind. Your will. The Spirit is waiting. He longs to intercede for you, if you will simply allow Him to do what He does best.

9

THE SEAL

Do you know the advertisement jingle "Plop, plop, fizz, fizz—oh, what a relief it is!"? That's from Alka Seltzer commercials where the medicinal tablets are dropped into water and transformation occurs. What was once water turns into an empowered liquid able to bring relief for heartburn, upset stomach, or indigestion. It's the indwelling of the tablets in the water that brings about the change.

The tablets are what they are even without being in the water. But when they indwell the water, they turn into a more viable solution to the problem of physical discomfort.

Every believer who has trusted Jesus Christ has plop, plop, fizz, fizz relief because they possess the Holy Spirit. The Holy Spirit is a new resident in an old house. This old house of our humanity, which over time is fading away, has now been indwelt with the person of the Spirit. The third member of the Trinity was placed into your life, dropped into your spirit in order to operate as a permanent part of your humanity from then on. His presence brings relief to life's disturbances and pains when you need it most.

This next name for the Holy Spirit emphasizes His role of indwelling.

Just as the tablets dropped into the water become a permanent portion of that water, so does the Holy Spirit become a permanent resident in each of us when we're saved. The name that teaches us this reality is the Seal, and we read about it in Ephesians 1:13-14:

> In Him, you also, after listening to the message of truth, the gospel of your salvation—having also believed, you were sealed in Him with the Holy Spirit of promise, who is given as a pledge of our inheritance, with a view to the redemption of God's own possession, to the praise of His glory.

As followers of Jesus Christ, we have been sealed with the Holy Spirit of promise. This seal is indicative of our relationship with God and results in the praise of His glory. As you might recall, the advancement of God's kingdom agenda on earth is all about promoting the glory of God. The Holy Spirit's permanent presence within us enables us to bring greater glory to God in all that we do.

THE SEALING PRESENCE OF THE SPIRIT

Three concepts are tied to this specific name of the sealing presence of the Spirit. The first concept is that it guarantees security. The second concept is that it establishes ownership. And the third is that it's reflective of authority. Thus the Seal outlines that which pertains to our security, ownership, and authorization.

1. The Seal Guarantees Security

When we're sealed with the Holy Spirit, He makes us secure in God forever. Ephesians 4:30 says it like this: "Do not grieve the Holy Spirit of God, by whom you were sealed for the day of redemption." The seal cannot be broken until redemption has occurred. You and I have been sealed for the day of redemption. The seal is there until redemption takes place. This reveals permanency to the Seal. In other words, you can't lose or undo your salvation.

Isn't it good to know you don't have to keep yourself saved? Once you've trusted in Jesus Christ, you've been born into the family of God. He has linked you to union with Christ in such a way that you can't be unlinked. Just as a person born into a family biologically can never undo their biological connection, when you're born into the family of God and sealed with the Spirit, you can never undo that spiritual connection.

I love the way Paul talks about this permanency in Romans 8:35-39:

> Who will separate us from the love of Christ? Will tribulation, or distress, or persecution, or famine, or nakedness, or peril, or sword? Just as it is written, "For Your sake we are being put to death all day long; we were considered as sheep to be slaughtered." But in all these things we overwhelmingly conquer through Him who loved us. For I am convinced that neither death, nor life, nor angels, nor principalities, nor things present, nor things to come, nor powers, nor height, nor depth, nor any other created thing, will be able to separate us from the love of God, which is in Christ Jesus our Lord.

In short, nothing can separate us from the love of Christ once we've been saved, which means you and I can live with the assurance and the security of the seal. Not even the devil can break this seal, despite what he tries to tell you. Since God is the One who sealed you, only He has the authority to remove that seal, and He's made it clear that it will not be removed until the day of redemption. God has secured both your salvation and your redemption.

People vacuum-seal an item or group of items, getting out all the air, because they want to extend the life of whatever is being sealed. In securing your salvation with redemption, God has extended your life even into eternity. Not only that, but the act of sealing is also designed to keep out contamination. Items are often sealed so bacteria can't get in and spoil them. Similarly, God has sealed your new nature with the Spirit so it can no longer be destroyed by the world, the flesh, or the devil.

2. The Seal Establishes Ownership

The name the Seal also indicates ownership. For example, in Jeremiah 32:9-10, we read how the prophet speaks of the process of sealing to establish ownership: "'I bought the field which was at Anathoth from Hanamel my uncle's son, and I weighed out the silver for him, seventeen shekels of silver. I signed and sealed the deed, and called in witnesses, and weighed out the silver on the scales.'"

In signing and sealing the deed, he established ownership over the property. In fact, many documents in our culture to this day have seals on them. We often establish both authenticity and ownership with a seal. If we buy a car, we place a seal on the title. When we get married, a seal is placed on the marriage license itself. Seals like these allow those who need to use such documents for processing other items can quickly identify that they're originals and not forged.

As children of the King, we've also been bought and thus sealed under the ownership of God. First Corinthians 6:19-20 puts it this way: "Do you not know that your body is a temple of the Holy Spirit who is in you, whom you have from God, and that you are not your own? For you have been bought with a price: therefore glorify God in your body."

You and I have been bought with a price—the high price of the atonement of Jesus Christ. The Holy Spirit's sealing of our souls establishes the reality that we are now owned by God. We are no longer to live as self-owned, autonomous individuals. Rather, we are to glorify God with our bodies—the bodies He purchased through the shed blood of His Son.

This area of ownership is one of the problems facing many Christians today. When believers live with the false ideology that they own their own lives, they get lost on the pathway. When they falsely believe they own their own material items, they use them in ways other than the expansion of God's kingdom on earth.

Yet as believers in Jesus Christ, we own nothing. That's why the Bible calls us stewards. We're blessed to use that which God provides, but we're to use it as stewards or managers. We're to do so under the guidance of the true Owner, God Himself. Through the seal of the Spirit, He both secures and owns us.

This is a critical life-forming principle, because if you insist on owning yourself, you will live in conflict with the actual Owner. God doesn't back down just because you say you want to own your life and material items. Rather, He often allows you to find out what that looks like. This leads to disastrous results, because whenever a steward starts to act as an owner, disaster follows.

The question you need to ask yourself as we study the names, descriptions, and attributes for the Holy Spirit as well as His impact in our lives is this: *Have I surrendered ownership to the Lord Jesus Christ so that the Spirit of God can do what He wants to do in my life?* The Holy Spirit is there to represent God the Father and Jesus the Son.

3. The Seal Reflects Authorization

Last, the Seal indicates authorization. When you receive a sealed, certified letter, the only person authorized to open the letter is you, the person to whom the letter was sent. The sender can open it if it's sent back, or the receiver can open it, but that's it. That's why we often have to show proof of identification when handed a sealed document—because the seal indicates authority must exist for it to be opened.

When Jesus Christ saved you and gave you the Holy Spirit, He gave you divine authorization to utilize the Spirit on your behalf. Other people can't utilize the Holy Spirit placed within you because they haven't been sealed with the Spirit in you. Further, only as believers in Jesus Christ does anyone receive the Seal.

This concept shows up regularly in Scripture. If we review a few of the passages, we'll gain greater insight into the authority of a seal.

Now you write to the Jews as you see fit, in the king's name, and seal it with the king's signet ring; for a decree which is written in the name of the king and sealed with the king's signet ring may not be revoked (Esther 8:8).

A stone was brought and laid over the mouth of the den; and the king sealed it with his own signet ring and with the signet rings of his nobles, so that nothing would be changed in regard to Daniel (Daniel 6:17).

I saw in the right hand of Him who sat on the throne a book written inside and on the back, sealed up with seven seals. And I saw a strong angel proclaiming with a loud voice, "Who is worthy to open the book and to break its seals?" And no one in heaven or on the earth or under the earth was able to open the book or to look into it (Revelation 5:1-3).

Seals indicate permanency of security, ownership, and authorization. They are no small thing throughout history and even now in contemporary times. Only God has the authority to break the seal of the Holy Spirit. Because of this, you now bear the authority of the One who has sealed you. No man can reverse it, including yourself. No demon can reverse it. Nobody can steal it from you, because you've been divinely authorized and sealed by God. The seal on you establishes your identity in relationship to the One who sealed you.

Now, as we've already seen throughout this book, you and I need to be filled with the Holy Spirit in order to gain access to all He has to offer us. We also need to walk in the Spirit as we live out our days. But regardless of how much interaction we have with the Spirit and how much we seek to maximize our lives in His strength, we are forever sealed by the Spirit. You can consider the Spirit like a deposit of things to come. We saw this earlier in Ephesians 1:13-14: "[The Holy Spirit]... is given as a pledge of our inheritance, with a view to the redemption of God's own possession, to the praise of His glory."

The Spirit has been sealed in us as a "pledge." Some Bible versions refer to this as a deposit. If you've purchased anything expensive in your life—like a house—you know it often comes with a down payment. The down payment means you're committed to the purchase with more of your commitment to come.

Some of you grew up in the day when S&H Green Stamps were given out to those making purchases at grocery stores, gas stations, and department stores. After collecting enough of these trading stamps for some item you wanted—perhaps a small kitchen appliance or a toy—and affixing them into provided "books," you could trade them for that item. The stamps acted like a pledge, promising you could visit an S&H Green Stamp redemption center and choose the item you wanted.

Before the onset of credit cards being in high use, many stores offered layaway plans. You could make a deposit on a product, then make frequent trips to the store to pay a portion of the amount required until it was finally paid for in full and you could take the item home.

Now, keep in mind, people made deposits only on items they planned to purchase. They didn't just run around putting deposits on every single thing they saw just because they liked it. Deposits indicated intention to buy. Just as S&H Green Stamps represented the promise of redemption at one of their centers.

God tells us the Holy Spirit being sealed inside of you is a deposit or pledge. It's the first installment on a layaway plan that involves eternity and is forever tied to your redemption. It's a pledge to complete your redemption.

When you accepted Jesus Christ, the Holy Spirit was sealed in you as a guarantee that God will finish this purchase and redemption. God has promised you glory. He has promised you heaven. He has promised you eternal peace, rest, and a reunification with your loved ones who have been saved and gone on to heaven ahead of you. But that promise doesn't happen immediately. It is the seal of the promise that happens immediately.

Let me illustrate it like this: When a woman receives an engagement ring from a suitor, that means he's decided to marry her. The ring symbolizes a pledge. It's a down payment of sorts, or a deposit, or a pledge. The ring says there's more to come. Whatever the gap of time may be from the moment the engagement ring is placed on her finger to the day of the wedding is simply a preparation gap for the ultimate goal.

God has given every believer an engagement ring. The seal of the Spirit is His pledge that indicates His intention for an ultimate marriage. In Scripture it's called the "marriage supper of the Lamb" (Revelation 19:9). That's when God will bring each of us to live with Him. In the meantime, you and I live in a space of time that's a preparation gap for what's to come.

Now, when that woman accepts the engagement ring, she shouldn't go out and date someone else. She should wear the ring proudly, letting other people know she's spoken for, now unavailable to anyone other than her husband-to-be. Her commitment has been determined. Unfortunately, though, far too many Christians who have received the seal of the Spirit go out and date the world. They still date the wisdom of this world order. They two-time or even three-time God all the while forgetting the price He paid to put the ring on their finger.

Can you imagine how a potential groom would feel or even act if his fiancée did that? Do you think he would still agree to all of the wedding plans and potential expenses for the event? Do you think he would want to hang out with the woman who was two-timing or even three-timing him? Do you think he would invest his time and energy into the relationship?

I don't. But that's similar to what happens to us when we're sealed in the Spirit but then two-time God. We wind up failing to maximize the purpose for the Spirit's place in our lives. We fail to maximize His relationship with us.

The good news about an engagement, though, is that you can start making plans. You can start preparing for the wedding ahead. Similarly, when we're sealed by the Spirit, we can also start making plans. We can plan for eternity.

Instead of living for today, you can look forward to the days before you. You can start thinking about what is to come and making decisions in alignment with that. When you focus on eternity, it affects your choices right now, just like when a couple is focused on their upcoming wedding it affects their spending and activities prior to the ceremony. Young couples will often save not only for a wedding but also for a house or furniture. A lot goes into joining two lives together, including the cost of a honeymoon.

We easily understand how future events impact present choices when it comes to things like getting married, buying a house, having children, or sending kids to college, so it shouldn't be hard to understand how living in light of eternity should influence our daily decisions. What you do now will last throughout eternity. What you do now matters. The seal of the Holy Spirit is a continual reminder of the promises to come. Yet if you don't have an eternal perspective, you will fail to maximize all the Spirit has been designed to provide.

Maximizing the Holy Spirit's role in your life equates to maximizing your life. Whenever the Holy Spirit is free to fully work both in and through you, you become empowered to live out your purpose and calling. And in doing these things, you find true satisfaction and joy.

Paul tells us about this as we continue our exploration of Ephesians 1:

> For this reason I too, having heard of the faith in the Lord Jesus which exists among you and your love for all the saints, do not cease giving thanks for you, while making mention of you in my prayers; that the God of our Lord Jesus Christ, the Father of glory, may give to you a spirit of wisdom and of revelation in the knowledge of Him. I pray that the eyes of your heart may be enlightened, so that you will know what is the hope of His calling, what

are the riches of the glory of His inheritance in the saints, and what is the surpassing greatness of His power toward us who believe (Ephesians 1:15-19).

The Holy Spirit will enable and empower you to know the hope of your calling. He will strengthen you to know the riches of the glory of the inheritance you're due as a follower of Jesus Christ.

THE HOLY SPIRIT ENLIGHTENS YOU

The Holy Spirit will also give you the ability to access the surpassing greatness of His power, and He does this by enlightening you. He informs your human spirit with His wisdom through the revelation and knowledge of Him. In doing so, you are released to experience more of God's reality in your life. You begin to see the things around you more clearly. As though glasses have been put on eyes grown weak, the images before you will take shape. The decisions you need to make will make sense. The courage required of you to walk by faith will be infused in you. You will gain clarity and conviction to live out the calling God has in store for your life.

We often get confused about what are the real problems in life and what are merely illusions of problems. This is because without tapping into the Holy Spirit's insight, we rely on our own spiritual eyes, which are darkened. When you fail to see things spiritually, you react to things physically. When you fail to trust in God's sovereignty, your body reacts with anxiety. When you fail to step out in faith, you backtrack in fear.

To perceive things spiritually and apply God's truth to that which you perceive is a gift of the Spirit's seal in your life. But this gift is accessed only when you acknowledge and live according to the other aspects of the seal—that of the ownership and authority of God over you.

God longs to work experientially in your life through the indwelling of the Holy Spirit. When that takes place, you'll see Him start showing up for you in ways you never anticipated. You'll get to see God's hand in your life moving and shifting things for you, opening doors you, again, didn't even know to knock on. This is because God sees all things. You and I see only what we can with our physical eyes. But when we learn to tap into the enlightenment of the Holy Spirit, we learn to see things spiritually.

This will have a positive impact on how you navigate the various vicissitudes of life. You will begin to discern whether something is truly good for you or actually bad for you. You'll be able to tell if God brought something to you all tied up with a nice bow or if Satan did. Satan is a master deceiver. Without the help of the Holy Spirit, even the smartest human will fall to his schemes. You and I have to walk in the enlightenment of the Holy Spirit to be able to differentiate between what is of God and what is of the devil simply made to look as if it's from God.

When you discover how to walk according to the illumination of spiritual eyes, you'll discover a life you only dreamed of before. Look all throughout the Bible for examples of this.

Joshua would normally have relied on a proven military strategy for taking on the city of Jericho, but God told him to have his men march around the city in order to make the walls fall down. That's not a great strategy, if you ask me. But it worked because it was God's method for winning that battle.

Gideon probably wanted all 30,000 of his men to go in and fight a battle in order to give him the odds he felt were comfortable enough to enter the war at all. But God instructed him to use 300 men instead. Gideon was able to obey God because he understood the difference between the spiritual and the physical.

Another example is Abraham. Abraham never would have come up with the idea of offering his son Isaac on that altar in hopes that God would somehow intervene at the last minute, offering instead a ram. But that's what God asked him to do, and he did it. As a result, Abraham continued to experience the full manifestation of the power of God in his life to do great things and be the father of many nations.

You and I can live in the physical according to our physical senses. We are given free will. If we want to remain autonomous, God gives us that choice. But if we do make that choice, we'll also be choosing to live life apart from spiritual enlightenment. Our choices and emotions will no doubt reflect this reality. Only when we allow all of the elements of the seal of the Holy Spirit to be fully expressed in our life will we tap into all of the benefits the Spirit is designed to supply.

Psalm 103:7 distinguishes between those who choose to walk in the physical and those who choose to walk in the spiritual: "He made known His ways to Moses, His acts to the sons of Israel." Moses saw the ways of God while Israel got to see only His acts.

To put it another way, Israel saw what God did. Moses saw who God is. He saw the why and the how behind what God did. He got more information than that of an observer. He was a participant in the mighty acts of God Himself.

WHAT WILL YOU CHOOSE?

So really, it depends on what you want out of life. Do you want to sit on the sidelines and watch what God does for other people? Or do you want to walk up the mountain to experience God, like Moses did, face-to-face? Do you want to be in the crowd, or do you want insider information? It really is your choice. God will never force you to walk according to His ways. But He will enable you to do so through the sealing of the Holy Spirit. What you do with His gift is entirely up to you.

When my son Jonathan was in college, he bred pit bulls. One day he brought three of them home. As you might guess, I wasn't about to let any of these canines in our house. So they had to stay out back tied to a lamppost.

Now, if you know anything about pit bulls, you know they have huge heads. Their heads are oversized compared to their bodies.

One morning when Jonathan went out to get the dogs ready for a walk, he discovered they had wrapped themselves around the post overnight so tightly that they could barely move. He had to spend an inordinate amount of time untangling them, literally walking them backward from where they'd once been. They had to go in reverse. They'd functioned according to their big heads and gone in a direction they never should have gone in at all. As a result, they needed to backtrack from any forward progress they'd thought they'd made.

Living with big heads like pit bulls has a biblical term that summarizes it: "Lean on your own understanding" (Proverbs 3:5). When you and I walk according to our own human wisdom, we discover that any progress we thought we made is quickly undone. Our own thoughts and decisions merely entangle us, causing us to be stuck. Then when God comes to free us so we can walk with the Spirit, we have to first go backward in order to undo the mess we've made.

You and I belong to Jesus Christ, and He has a good plan for our lives. But we'll experience this plan only when we allow the Holy Spirit to fully express Himself inside our lives. Instead of leaning on our own understanding, we are to look to Him, listen to Him, and go where He leads us. Not only are we sealed for eternity by the power of the Spirit within, but when we sync up with the Holy Spirit in our everyday activities and thoughts, we're enabled to live out the full manifestation of our calling and purpose on earth.

10

THE BREATH

We became all too familiar with the phrase *I can't breathe* in 2020. While the words came literally attached to the deaths of Eric Garner and George Floyd, the refrain itself arose to symbolically describe the historical oppression of a group of people. Shirts, posters, hats, chants—you name it—held up this phrase over and over again for the world to see. It took on its own meaning as it grew into a worldwide movement.

What's more, as the COVID-19 pandemic continued to display its ugly claws on society's stage, many more people lost their lives through their inability to breathe. The struggle for breath was a challenge so many faced—and on so many levels. If you didn't face it yourself, you probably know someone who did.

We all know how serious these words are. The inability to breathe means life is in jeopardy. Conversely, the ability to breathe means we're able to take in life and are free to live. Breath matters. It matters for good and it's terribly detrimental when the ability to do it is lost. That's why this next name for the Holy Spirit is so important. The Bible refers to the Spirit as the Breath. He is literally the oxygen of God.

Many Scriptures bring this out, but the meaning remains the same no matter what the context. When you and I understand that the Spirit is our oxygen—our ability to breathe spiritually—we can fully grasp that He is our very ability to live.

Spiritual life and death in the physical realm are tied to our relationship to the Holy Spirit because that is the relationship we have to breathe. To the degree we're breathing the Holy Spirit on a regular basis, is the degree to which we're able to experience the life and presence of God in our midst. It's also the degree to which we experience hope in the midst of the hopelessness.

Have you heard this story about a doctor giving a patient the results of some tests he'd run? He said, "I have some bad news, and I also have some really bad news. What do you want to hear first?"

The patient responded, "The bad news."

"Based on your test results, you have only 24 hours to live."

The patient sat there stunned, then asked, "So what's the really bad news, then?"

"Well, unfortunately, the really bad news is I should have told you that yesterday."

It's a made-up story, but you get the point. Things can really go from bad to worse quickly. Just as the physical respiratory system can be in trouble when a sickness or restraint comes along, making it difficult to breathe, so can our spiritual respiratory system get in trouble when we fail to take in the breath of the Spirit Himself.

We read about this unique yet powerful name of the Holy Spirit in John 20:19-22:

> When it was evening on that day, the first day of the week, and when the doors were shut where the disciples were, for fear of the Jews, Jesus came and stood in their midst and said to them, "Peace be with you." And when He had said this, He showed them both His hands and His side. The disciples then rejoiced when they saw the Lord. So Jesus

said to them again, "Peace be with you; as the Father has sent Me, I also send you." And when He had said this, He breathed on them and said to them, "Receive the Holy Spirit."

THE BREATH OF GOD

Jesus transferred the Holy Spirit to the disciples through His breath. He breathed on them. And when He did that, they breathed in the Spirit. The Hebrew word in the Old Testament for the breath of God, which is the Spirit of God, is *ruach*. We see this in Genesis 2:7: "Then the LORD God formed man of dust from the ground, and breathed into his nostrils the breath of life; and man became a living being."

Just as God had used the Spirit as His breath hovering over creation and bringing life out of chaos in Genesis 1, He used the Spirit to breathe into the dirt itself as He formed man. In this way, Adam became a living soul. The *ruach* is the breath of God that gives life. When Jesus was talking with Nicodemus in John 3:5-8, He referred to this new life the Spirit brings. He let us know this same truth in John 6:63: "It is the Spirit who gives life; the flesh profits nothing; the words that I have spoken to you are spirit and are life."

The New Testament word for the Spirit here is *pneuma*. In fact, that's where we get our contemporary English term, *pneumonia*. As you can see, we have directly tied a word indicating a failure or difficulty to breathe due to sickness to the original term, which spoke of the Spirit. Both the Old Testament and the New Testament clearly link the Spirit to the Breath of life itself. Without the presence of the Spirit of God, you are not a living being. You may be physically alive, but you are spiritually dead.

That's why Ephesians 2:1 describes what happens in the presence of sin as being "dead in your trespasses." Without the Spirit pulsating the oxygen of the life of God within us, we can't truly live. We can't experience the life Jesus spoke of in John 10:10: "The thief comes only to steal and kill and destroy; I came that they may have life, and have it abundantly." Thus, the more of the Holy Spirit you inhale, the more life of God you experience. You must have the life of God in order to live out the abundance Jesus speaks of. When you do, you're positioned to take part in the highest possible level of the spiritual realm while on earth.

The breath of God is the Spirit of God at work. Job spoke of it like this: "The Spirit of God has made me, and the breath of the Almighty gives me life" (Job 33:4). The breath of God is the Spirit of God. The Spirit of God is the breath of God. When God exhales, it is the Spirit going to work. God doesn't just exhale in order to exhale; He exhales life into His creation because the Spirit gives life.

One of the problems that runs rampant in our Christian culture today is a lack of Holy Spirit oxygen. Christians are not breathing in the Holy Spirit, and so they have no spiritual oxygen circulating in them. Just as the physical body begins to break down without oxygen, the spiritual life does as well. All manner of issues arise in the absence of oxygen.

In the physical, it leads to organ failure. In the spiritual, it leads to life failure, whether that shows up in anxiety, depression, irritability, vitriol, despondency, or an incessant searching for hedonistic pleasures. We can't expect to thrive without the oxygen of the Spirit. For some reason, we understand this concept in the physical world and take measures to ensure our oxygen flows, but when it comes to our souls, we often somehow think we can wing it.

Yet God is the life within us. Without Him, we merely exist. We, like Dr. Frankenstein's monster, may have the anatomy of a human being, but without a fully healthy soul we are anything but alive. For too many people, this results in monstrous behavior in attitudes and actions, character and conduct, because they have access to the body but without the life to guide it to its proper use.

One occupation you will never see me in is that of a mortician. I just won't do it. One reason is I don't want to spend my life in the midst of the dead. But another reason is that a friend who was a mortician told me something that changed how I would view that profession forever.

Sometimes when a mortician is working on a cadaver, it will move. The body will twitch. Or the cadaver will even blink. Muscular reaction can still exist. One time my friend even had a cadaver literally twitch itself off the table and onto the floor. That would have to happen to me only once before I never stepped foot in that mortuary again. Either that, or there would quickly be two cadavers on the floor, one of them mine! That's just not my thing.

But the point I saw in this man's story resonated with me spiritually as well. People can be spiritually anatomically correct. They can go to church, say their prayers, and read their Bible but still lack spiritual breath. In a sense, the spiritual body is carrying out twitches—spiritual reactions we've been designed to do but have no real life at all.

Psalm 104:30 tells us how God makes us alive: "You send forth Your Spirit, they are created; and You renew the face of the ground." We are alive when the Spirit's breath is within us. Even non-Christians benefit from the Spirit's breath, because His breath brings to life the physical, created order as well. But without His spiritual breath circulating within the physical body after creation, we are merely men and women in bodies. We only access and maximize spiritual life when we stay tied to the ongoing flow of the Spirit.

BREATHE OUT FEAR

In the passage in John 20, Jesus had just walked through a door. Not through a doorway. Through a literal door. He could do this because He was in His glorified body and no longer tied to physical limitations on earth.

When Jesus approached the disciples, they were already huddled together in fear. They were afraid of those who had killed Jesus, and they worried that the Jews may also come for them. That's why they had the door bolted shut. That's why they couldn't breathe. Fear will do that to you. It will take the breath right out of you.

Today we're living in a world full of fear with a lot to fear. We're afraid of human diseases like cancer. We're afraid of viruses like COVID-19. We're afraid to travel, afraid to shake hands, afraid when someone sneezes. We're afraid of violence. We're afraid of racial strife. We're afraid of verbal abuse, which has risen to a near cultural norm. We're afraid of the next storm. Afraid of the next war or even the potential of nuclear attack. Just turn on the news for one minute, and you'll find a list of things to fear.

As a result, our breathing is more shallow. This happens anytime we're afraid. We probably don't do it consciously, but when fear takes over, our breathing is affected. That's why so many people tell those who are afraid and panicking, "Breathe." The very act of breathing deeply and circulating oxygen throughout the body helps to readjust the body's focus and bring calm back into form.

Jesus didn't tell the disciples to breathe deeply when He walked through that door and found them huddled in fear. But He did tell them something similar in their cultural context. He said, "Peace be with you." He knew they were scared. He could see they were terrified. Their lives were in danger, after all. But when Jesus showed up, He took a moment to remind them to breathe. He did this by dialing down their fear. And then He breathed on them. He imparted the life of the Spirit into them through breath in order to calm their fears even more.

This is exactly what Jesus does in our lives as well. He stands at the door of our hearts and knocks, waiting for us to let Him in (Revelation 3:20). When we do, He brings peace with Him. And as we look to Him, the Spirit of life is breathed into our hearts, calming us from fear. This is carried out through a variety of ways, such as when we engage with the Word of God, which is the word of life. The Word of God gives life.

In 2 Timothy 3:16, the Bible says, "All Scripture is inspired by God." The Greek word in that passage is *theopneustos,* which means "to breathe out." This lets us know that Scripture is the Holy Spirit. It's the inspired Spirit of God in print.

Second Peter 1:20-21 explains it like this:

> Know this first of all, that no prophecy of Scripture is a matter of one's own interpretation, for no prophecy was ever made by an act of human will, but men moved by the Holy Spirit spoke from God.

THE SPIRIT OF GOD CONNECTED TO THE WORD OF GOD

The Bible is the voice of God in print—the Spirit's breath written down in such a way that we can take it in and live by it. Which is why whenever you separate the Word of God from a relationship with God, it may not have the life-giving effect of the Spirit on you that you hoped it would. You need a relationship with God for His words to take life in you. You want the living Word to be connected to the written Word so that the breath of God's Spirit can bring life into your dryness, circumstances, situations, and environment (Ezekiel 37:1-14). The Spirit is the oxygen tank that secures our survival in the waters of a wicked world.

Until the Spirit becomes an active, life-giving supplier of the Word of God into our mind, heart, and spirit, we'll continue to struggle in every way. We'll continue to have people who can't breathe or are struggling to breathe spiritually seeking to get along with others who are struggling just as hard.

If you've ever witnessed someone struggling to breathe in person or seen a character struggling in a drowning scene on television or in a film, you know they lash out. They don't behave the way they normally do. Something similar happens to us when we can't breathe spiritually. Our traumas, our pain, our struggles, and our fears cause us to lash out at others. As you can quickly surmise, it's difficult for people to get along when they're lashing out, trying to breathe spiritually.

Only when the Spirit of God connects with the Word of God because it is tied to the person of God are we able to breathe. As spiritual breath enters our system, we can think and speak and behave in ways that are conducive to bringing health and healing in relationships as well. When the Word of God is living within us through the breath of the Spirit, it begins to manifest its results in our lives. In other words, it becomes more than words on paper or a digital device; it becomes an experience.

The job of the Holy Spirit is to take the still photograph of the Word of God and turn it into a motion picture. If you've seen the film *The Passion of the Christ*, you clearly know the difference between reading about the crucifixion and seeing it portrayed. I had read about it countless times, even preached about it. But when I saw that film, the crucifixion scenes left a significantly stronger imprint on my heart. I wasn't just reading about Christ's suffering and death, and I wasn't just understanding it. I was experiencing it as much as I possibly could experience something that happened more than 2,000 years ago.

I get it. Sometimes the Bible can seem like a dead book. Like it's just full of stories that took place so long ago that they have no relevance to today. But the Bible is not a dead book. Scripture is clear that the Bible is alive (Hebrews 4:12). And because it's alive with the breath of the Spirit infused in it, it can be made to come alive in our own experiences as well.

It won't do that simply by our reading it, though. You and I don't possess the power to make it alive in our hearts and minds. The Holy Spirit breathes life into the pages for us.

GOD GIVES YOU A CHOICE

But the Holy Spirit will give you only as much oxygen as you allow, just like a faucet gives you only the amount of water that can flow based on how far you've turned it. The Holy Spirit has all the oxygen you need for the Scriptures to be fully alive in your spirit, but He can allow only the amount you allow in to flow. It's a relationship. You have a choice. You have free will. You are not forced to inhale spiritual oxygen on a ventilator. God has given each of us a choice.

Once again we look to Galatians 5. Verse 25 puts it like this: "If we live by the Spirit, let us also walk by the Spirit." Walking is something you do, not something done to you. Walking is an action you take. Nobody walks for you. When you breathe the oxygen of the Holy Spirit, you similarly must choose how deep a breath to take. He is the life-Source to each of us as believers, but you and I must choose to inhale deeply and frequently in order to experience the full benefit of what He has to offer.

In other words, God doesn't want you simply visiting the Spirit; He wants you relying on Him. He doesn't want you to pray only when you're about to eat a meal; He wants you to pray always. He doesn't want you to just read a Bible verse or two or even a whole chapter; He wants you to meditate on His Word. He doesn't want to merely be your life coach; He wants to be your God.

Let me ask you a question to consider. When you breathe, do you inhale and hold it? Do you take one breath and then go about your business for the day? Or do you breathe, let the breath out; breathe again, let the breath out again; and so forth all day long? Of course you do the latter. One breath just won't do it for much longer than a minute. It's the way we've been designed. In fact, we don't even need to think about it. Most of us breathe without thinking. We breathe without effort. That's how God wants our relationship to be when we rely on the Holy Spirit for the spiritual oxygen we need.

We are to breathe in concert with the Spirit so that it becomes second nature to us. We are to reflect His thoughts in our hearts and minds without having to make any effort to do so. It should be natural to us. We are to walk so closely with Him that His breath is a natural extension of our own. His voice is a natural part of our own. His leading is naturally taken into consideration in every decision we make. We shouldn't have to think too hard to consult the Spirit, because when

He's an ongoing part of our everyday lives, He's so near that He's advising and guiding us without our even having to ask Him to.

OVERCOMING CHAOS, GAINING PEACE

When we live and breathe like that, we have everything we need to overcome all that comes at us. Jesus tells us, "These things I have spoken to you, so that in Me you may have peace. In the world you have tribulation, but take courage; I have overcome the world" (John 16:33). Jesus always spoke peace to pervade the fear consuming those He loved. He told them, and subsequently us, that He wanted them to experience His peace.

God doesn't want you to succumb to the chaos around you. You may not be able to stop the chaos, sure. You may not be able to change the chaos itself. But you no longer need to be controlled by it. Once the chaos controls you, you've lost your peace. You've lost the overcoming power of the presence of the Spirit of God. And just like how breathing becomes shallow in proximity to fear, your spiritual life becomes shallow in the presence of fear as well when you focus on the chaos rather than on Christ.

In Mark 4:35-41, we're told the story about the disciples crossing the Sea of Galilee with Jesus. Jesus was asleep when a windstorm came up and began tossing their boat around like a child's toy. And despite the disciples being burly men for their day, they quickly became afraid. Yet in the midst of their fear, Jesus still slept. Scripture tells us He even had His head on a pillow, no doubt sleeping well.

When the disciples woke Him because they were afraid they were about to die, Jesus chastised them for their little faith. He did that because when they got on the boat, He told them they were going to the other side. He'd told them the end from the beginning. Yet the disciples chose to trust what they were experiencing on the sea rather than what they heard from Jesus Himself.

Fear will do that. Fear will cause you to forget God's Word faster than much of anything other than fear itself.

Jesus didn't tell the disciples, "Let's go halfway across the sea and drown." No, He told them clearly that they were going to the other side. But they forgot this in the face of their fears. So instead of relying on faith to see them through the wind and the waves, they relied on their own human perspective. As a result, their fear only got worse until Jesus finally had to get up and command the storm to be still. He said, "Peace, be still," and the storm was.

One of the reasons we can't seem to breathe so easily anymore is that the Word of God has become rare to us. Yes, we open our Bibles when the preacher gives us a Scripture or we don't know what to do in various situations, but we no longer consume the Word of God, breathe it in, abide in it, and meditate on it as we've been instructed to do. When the Word is no longer the air we breathe, our spiritual health suffers and we experience spiritual asthma attacks.

When I was working on my Bible commentary, I spent an inordinate amount of time combing through Psalm 119 because it's the longest chapter in the Bible. I couldn't just read it and give a summary. I needed to understand its ins and outs in order to give both a holistic overview and a deep dive into its meaning.

One thing stood out to me: The Word of God is life itself. Everything originates from, gets its order from, and is led toward the Word of God. If you want to experience the peace of God that is yours when you need it most, you must draw close to the Spirit of God in concert with the Word of God. When these two are working in tandem in your heart and mind, you will have peace.

If you're in a bad situation, have no hope, and can't seem to find God anywhere, know that He has not gone away. You have. So check yourself. Check where you are in relation to His Spirit's truth within you and in relation to His Word. Our world and our lives do not need to be in the crisis we're experiencing if we will only rely on God. It seems as if we're in a crisis loop. Chaos after chaos and conflict after conflict...all of it combined is seeking to take our breath away.

But when God allows pain, fear, and difficulties, remember He always has a purpose—for us to know He is the Lord. In Zechariah 4:6 He explains, "'Not by might nor by power, but by My Spirit.'" God's Spirit is who gives us the power we need to overcome anything. Politicians don't have the last say. Revolutionaries don't have the last say. Even your boss doesn't have the last say. It is God who speaks in such a way that creation listens. It is God who supplies all you need to live your life to the fullest. It is God who opens the doors you don't even know to knock on.

And He does this through the abiding presence of the Spirit within you. He infuses you with the oxygen of His life so you can make a spiritual impact as you follow Him and demonstrate to a watching world what living by faith truly means.

11

THE POWER

I'm sure you agree that electricity is one of the most powerful and beneficial forces available to us. Our homes are heated or cooled because of it. We're able to conveniently cook meals, refrigerate perishable food, and wash and dry clothes because of it. We can do so much more now than people who lived in the days before electricity was introduced into our world could. Without this power source, managing and maintaining our homes, businesses, and churches would be a lot more challenging.

Yes, electricity has revolutionized how we live, and it's all due to power we get from an invisible force.

You don't have to see something for it to provide immense benefit to your life. None of us can see wind, yet wind influences much of what we do. None of us can see electricity, yet electricity empowers much of what we do. None of us see the Holy Spirit, yet the Holy Spirit gives life to all we do.

JESUS LEAVES BEHIND THE HOLY SPIRIT

This name for the Holy Spirit—the Power—describes an attribute of His that's important for us to understand and tap into. We discover it in the book of Acts, where we read about the period of time shortly after Jesus rose from the dead. He had reached the conclusion of the 40-day window between His resurrection and His ascension, and during these last moments, He met with His followers to talk about what would happen when He left and to share more about the concepts in the kingdom of God.

In the midst of this conversation, Jesus pointed the disciples' thoughts and hearts toward the Holy Spirit. We read about it in Acts 1:6-8:

> When they had come together, they were asking Him, saying, "Lord, is it at this time You are restoring the kingdom to Israel?" He said to them, "It is not for you to know times or epochs which the Father has fixed by His own authority; but you will receive power when the Holy Spirit has come upon you; and you shall be My witnesses both in Jerusalem, and in all Judea and Samaria, and even to the remotest part of the earth."

The disciples wanted to know when Jesus would be returning to set up His kingdom, and He told them it was not for them to know. God wasn't revealing that information at that time. But He did want them to know that even though He was leaving them in His physical presence, He was still going to share His power with them. When He ascended into heaven, He'd leave behind the person of the Holy Spirit, who would transfer His spiritual power both to them and to each of us.

This attribute of power is one of the most misunderstood and underutilized aspects of the Holy Spirit. The Holy Spirit is a powerful member of the Trinity. He takes from God the power that is God's and delivers it to you and me so that the power of heaven is made available to us in history.

While Jesus spoke of the kingdom and God's kingdom agenda, which is the visible manifestation of the comprehensive rule of God over every area of life, He also let the disciples know that the return of this kingdom would have to wait for some time. In the meantime, though, His followers were to be vested with the power to carry out God's kingdom agenda while on earth. And in essence, when Jesus did that, through the Holy Spirit, He supplied us with kingdom electricity to bring about God's overarching goal in history.

THE HOLY SPIRIT AS IGNITOR, CHARGER, AND CONNECTOR

I once had a problem with the heating unit in my home. It wasn't working, it was in the dead of winter, and I was freezing. I called in a repair person and told him I thought I needed a new heating unit altogether. I assumed the whole thing was broken. But he took one look at my unit and said, "It's fine. Your ignitor just went out." It was a simple fix to a huge problem. All he needed to do was light a small piece of equipment inside the unit, which then lit the pilot so the flame could flow.

The Holy Spirit is our ignitor. He must be lit and allowed to burn fully within us in order for us to experience His power. No amount of church attendance, Bible study, attending small groups, or reading devotions will place you on the pathway of your kingdom purpose if the ignitor of the Holy Spirit has gone out. The Holy Spirit is responsible for empowering you to display the power within you.

Have you ever been left on the side of the road because your car battery went dead? That happened to me once. I'll never forget standing there with my car's hood up. After a while, someone kind stopped and offered to jump-start my car. He took the jumper cables from his own car and hooked them up to mine in order to transfer power. Even though I possessed the manual that explained what I needed to do when my car battery died, I couldn't revive it with information alone. My car wasn't about to move until someone transferred the power I needed.

The Bible contains all of the information we need in order to live our lives to the full. But if we're not properly hooked up to the Holy Spirit, it won't mean anything. We won't be able to go anywhere. Information without power is just information. The Holy Spirit must supply the power we need in order to enable us to use it. Without Him, we are spiritually stuck.

Have you ever been spiritually stuck? You can look at your life and not see any improvement or maturing process. You just remain stagnant. This is because you've been disconnected from the Holy Spirit's power. I'm not saying He's no longer there, because He lives inside of you. But the cables that once connected you so His power could flow through—the cables of communion and abiding with Him—have come undone.

Have you ever seen a rowboat trying to pull somebody on water skis? I'm sure you haven't. Neither have I. Even if a rowboat had eight people in it, they wouldn't have enough rowing power to get someone up out of the water in order to ski. The person on the skis would keep going under the water each time they tried because they weren't hooked up to the right power source.

When Jesus ascended to heaven and left His followers on earth, He left us the *dunamis*. This is the word the original Greek uses to describe the power He left behind in the person of the Spirit. The word *dunamis* may sound familiar to you because it's the word from which we derive our English word *dynamite*. The Holy Spirit is not simply a trickling of power to give us a little boost. He contains so much power that Jesus described Him as dynamite. That's explosive power. That's life-changing power. In fact, that's world-changing power.

YOUR NEW IDENTITY

If you want to take an even deeper look at the battery source every Christian has been given, look at Acts 1:5: "John baptized with water, but you will be baptized with the Holy Spirit not many days from now." This brings in the theology found in the doctrine of the baptism of the

Holy Spirit. The Greek word *baptizo* speaks of something being identified. Here's an illustration: A woman wants to make a pink dress for her daughter, so she takes some cloth that is not pink to a dye-maker. He dips the cloth in pink dye. When this takes place, the cloth has been reidentified. It now identifies with the pink color it was dipped in.

To be baptized is to reidentify yourself as a follower of Jesus Christ. Water baptism is simply a visible modeling of spiritual baptism. It publicly states that you want to be known as a follower of Jesus Christ, that you're willing to make yourself known by whom you choose to follow.

Now, baptism doesn't save you, as is evidenced by Jesus saying the thief on the cross next to Him was saved though, obviously, he never had the opportunity to be baptized. The gospel saves you (1 Corinthians 15:1-2). But once you are saved, God expects you to move into discipleship through your public identification with Jesus Christ. You are buried with Jesus symbolically in baptism when you go under the water, then raised to walk in the newness of life. God expects every Christian to be baptized because they are entering into a new relationship with a new King and a new kingdom.

The kingdom includes the rule of God over every area of life. God desires that we live our days promoting His rule on earth. This can only be done when we do so in the power the Holy Spirit supplies. We are commissioned to go out and advance God's kingdom, but we are to do so only in the strength of the Spirit. Luke 24:49 puts it like this: "And behold, I am sending forth the promise of My Father upon you; but you are to stay in the city until you are clothed with power from on high."

Just as in Acts, Luke retained the warning not to go ahead and do the work of the kingdom until the power of the Spirit came upon them. Luke used the word *clothed* to describe this. What do you do with clothing? You wear it. God expects you to wear Jesus Christ through the presence of the Spirit. Galatians 3:27 states it this way: "All of you who were baptized into Christ have clothed yourselves with Christ."

Clothing is a great identifier of people. You can tell what football team players are on by the uniforms they wear or what branch of military service people serve in by the clothing they're required to don. And you don't have to guess whether someone is an officer of the law, a doctor, or a judge. Their clothing lets you know. Clothing tells us a lot about a person.

As Christians, we are to be clothed in Christ. We are to wear His character, attributes, and qualities in such a way that they publicly identify us as His followers. In other words, there should be no question about to whom you belong or whose team you represent. Baptism indicates that you are a visible, identifiable kingdom disciple. When you commit to this and walk in the truth of what baptism represents, you will experience the Spirit's power. The job of the Holy Spirit is to take heaven's power and bring it to earth in order to strengthen you to carry out God's will. In this way, God will become visible through you.

A NEW WAY TO OPERATE

Prior to the COVID-19 pandemic, you would not have caught me anywhere near a computer. I didn't own one, and I had no plans to obtain one. But then I became a professional Zoom-ologist like so many others! I had to conduct our meetings for the church and the national ministry over this software called Zoom. Do you know what Zoom does? It takes the verbal and makes it visual. It turns a phone call into a video call. And now not only can you see the person you're talking to but you can add multiple people to one call. In this way, we were able to convene meetings and even church services and special prayer services during the pandemic lockdown.

The Holy Spirit is like our spiritual Zoom software. His job is to make visible that which we read in the Bible. His power brings the words to life both in and through us.

When Jesus preached on the kingdom before He left earth, He proclaimed a new standard. He set forth a new way of thinking. He spoke of the rule of God over all, and this rule was to govern believers' lives until His return. It would be different from what the disciples were used to because God's kingdom is a different realm. It's an entirely different worldview. It's a different way of talking, walking, thinking, acting, relating, and perceiving.

The problem, though, is that the power needed to fully function in this new realm comes from within the realm itself. We have access to the power only through Jesus Christ. He is the key. He is the cornerstone. He is the entry point into this different way of living.

But what Jesus provides as the entry point is not entirely what we need to operate. Jesus connects each of us with the Holy Spirit in order for us to access the power we need to carry out our lives in this kingdom realm. The degree to which we stay connected to the Spirit's power is the degree to which we're able to take this new worldview of the kingdom and infuse it into the culture and world in which we live.

We are to bring in what the King says about every subject, whether it's race, culture, class, gender, work, money, politics, or any other subject. Rather than rely on the old way of thinking and operating, we are now to provide this new way of thinking to every topic. In this manner, we influence those around us and all these arenas with a kingdom perspective.

But if we try to do this without the power of the Holy Spirit, we find ourselves defeated every time. We continue to live in confusion and chaos. Only when we are empowered to live out kingdom principles do we become an asset in promoting God's worldview throughout the various realms around us.

When you and I became Christians, we entered into a new set of rules and expectations. We entered into God's kingdom—His way of operating. And just as anyone who owns a home has a set way of operating there and asks visitors to abide by their rules, God also has a set way of functioning in His kingdom.

For example, if you're used to smoking and you visit my home, you won't find any ashtrays around. You'll have to smoke outside. That's because it's my home, and I have a set of rules even for those who visit. And even if you're used to using profanity, in my home, profanity doesn't fly. You'll have to adjust to my rules because it's my home. Most people don't have an issue with that when they visit someone else's house. They understand that's just the way it is.

When you became a Christian, you entered into God's kingdom. You entered into a kingdom with rules. If you don't like the rules, you can always go create your own world and run your own kingdom. But in this one, God's rules reign supreme.

Yet regardless of this reality, many people have brought the world's way of thinking and way of operating into God's kingdom and asked God to adjust. They are literally challenging God's standards and His rules in His world and in His kingdom, as if they know more than He does. As a result, we have the hot mess we see all around us, and we see little power emanating from us and through us.

THE IMPORTANCE OF SURRENDER

One of the reasons people challenge God's way of operating is that it's natural to seek to live from their own power. When we do that, we feel like we're in control. For most of us, to yield—or surrender—our power so the Holy Spirit's power can have full effect in our life is hard. It's an act of faith. It isn't something we take for a test drive to decide whether we like it. The power of the Holy Spirit, then, is given to us when we yield, not when we want to try it on for size. Thus, a lot of people miss out on a life lived out in the supernatural power of God because they won't take the step of faith to experience it.

Only when you yield will you get the inside scoop on how the Spirit's power can be made manifest in your life. Jesus spoke of it like this in John 16:12-15:

> I have many more things to say to you, but you cannot bear them now. But when He, the Spirit of truth, comes, He will guide you into all the truth; for He will not speak on

His own initiative, but whatever He hears, He will speak; and He will disclose to you what is to come. He will glorify Me, for He will take of Mine and will disclose it to you. All things that the Father has are Mine; therefore I said that He takes of Mine and will disclose it to you.

Whatever God is doing in His kingdom is disclosed to you through the Spirit of truth. You will know all you need to know in order to successfully navigate your life on earth through the power of intimate disclosure. The Father discloses it to the Son. The Son discloses it to the Spirit. The Spirit then discloses it to you. Like computers networked together, you will gain power through your access to the mind of God.

But this comes only when you're plugged in. If you're not in sync with the Spirit, you won't receive the flow of His power. If you're not operating on the Word of God in your everyday life, you're not operating on truth. You can call on the Holy Spirit all you want, but the moment you detour from Scripture, you have canceled the transfer of His power. The Spirit deals only with the truth of God. As John 17:17 says, "Sanctify them in the truth; Your word is truth."

Far too many Christians live without spiritual power because they have either left the truth or they're seeking to mix the truth with their own thoughts or the world's wisdom. Yet truth is canceled when it's merged with anything else. As Jesus said to the Pharisees in Mark 7:13, we can actually invalidate the Word of God by "tradition."

Did you know you can cancel the Bible in terms of how it operates in your life? You can cancel its power in your life. You can cancel its influence in your life. You can cancel the blessings that can come to you through the power of the covenant. You do all of this when you seek to merge secular thinking with God. You do this when you seek to merge worldly wisdom with God. You do this when you seek to merge your own "truth" with God's absolute truth. You cancel yourself. You cancel the power you could have gained through the Spirit's free flow in your soul.

The Holy Spirit's goal is not to make a big deal about you. The Holy Spirit's goal is not to make a big deal about our culture or spiritual celebrity influencers. Neither is it the Holy Spirit's goal to make a big deal about Himself. The Holy Spirit's goal is to make a big deal about Jesus Christ. That's why we're told time and again that our role on earth is to abide in Christ. Our role on earth is to be identified with Jesus. Our role is to be clothed with Christ. Our role is to glorify God and advance His kingdom by glorifying Jesus Christ. When we make Him known in all we say and do, we accomplish that goal.

The Holy Spirit will empower the amplification of Jesus Christ in your life. He will get behind that, and you won't even have to ask. When He sees you doing that, you'll be infused with more power, more wisdom, and more strength. The intentional pursuit of Jesus is what turns on the ignition of the power of the Spirit in your life.

Your connection to Christ is what engages the Holy Spirit not only in talk but also in walk. The power switch slides to full power when you live as a visible, verbal kingdom follower of the Lord Jesus Christ. The word *glorify* means to put something on display. It means to highlight it. To glorify means to exclaim in a way that is unmistakable. Our role as the church collectively and as Christians individually is to glorify Jesus Christ as we advance the kingdom of God. It's pretty straightforward. Thus, if you're not cultivating your relationship with Jesus, you're not accessing the power of the kingdom.

We make this too hard sometimes. We make "Holy Spirit hunting" our goal and complicate things too much. We make it about so much it was never about at all. Simply request the presence and power of the Holy Spirit in you on a continuous basis (Luke 11:13). Glorify Jesus, identify with Jesus, and abide in Jesus, and you will have the fullest expression of the Holy Spirit in your life any human being can. The more you align with Christ based on His Word, the more power you will have in your life. In fact, you'll have so much power that it will overflow naturally as you become His witness to others (Acts 1:8).

You won't even have to try to be a witness for Jesus. It will be natural for you. Just as it's natural for a couple to wear their wedding rings when they get married because they want to publicly identify with each other, it will be natural for you in all you say and do to be publicly identified with Jesus Christ. Sharing the gospel will come naturally to you. Living out the love of Jesus Christ will come naturally to you. You will not have to be forced or cajoled into representing Jesus when you have identified with Him.

What's more, when the Spirit sees you walking in step with the calling of the kingdom, He will empower you. He will lift you. He will open doors for you. He will enable you to do so much more than you could ever do on your own. The Spirit will act as helium in your lungs, lifting you out of your defeats, addictions, and despondency and placing you on a platform of spiritual influence and impact in the spheres you represent. You will live out your kingdom purpose when you learn to live according to the power of the Spirit made manifest in your life.

12

THE WIND AND FIRE

Depending on your age and background, you may be familiar with songs like "Let's Groove," "Serpentine Fire," and "Got to Get You Into My Life." The band whose hits they were, Earth, Wind & Fire, entered the music scene in the '70s and captured the attention of the R&B world with their unique sound and rhythm.

We're told that when Maurice White, the originator of the group, was thinking about what to call the band, he looked to astrology. Sagittarius, the sign of the elements, led him to Earth, Wind & Fire. He wanted a name that would let everyone know how strong the band's "electricity" was—so strong that it would both affect and infect the environment around them to such a degree that it could not be ignored. People wouldn't be able to look away. The band's presence would shake things up, light things up, and flow so forcefully through the air that no one would go untouched by it.

And much to his hopes and dreams, such was the case during their massive string of hits.

Such was the case for the Holy Spirit when He showed up on the scene for the early church. His appearance and presence were so powerful that He ignited something within these church founders and early members that would not only turn Jerusalem on its heels but go on to engulf the entire globe.

THE DAY OF PENTECOST

We read about this unique entrance of the Holy Spirit, which launched the church age, in Acts 2:1-4:

> When the day of Pentecost had come, they were all together in one place. And suddenly there came from heaven a noise like a violent rushing wind, and it filled the whole house where they were sitting. And there appeared to them tongues as of fire distributing themselves, and they rested on each one of them. And they were all filled with the Holy Spirit and began to speak with other tongues, as the Spirit was giving them utterance.

The Holy Spirit is the real Wind and Fire, which heaven brought down to consume the scene. He arrived at a time in history when the Israelites were having a big party, celebrating the giving of the Ten Commandments to Moses. This was the fiftieth day after the Passover, and they called this celebration *Pentecost*. Pentecost marked the remembrance of God's deliverance of Israel from Egypt as well as His giving of the law. But as time would play out, this special celebration would not only reflect on an historical reality but inaugurate the beginning of the formalized church.

To get the context of the Spirit's coming, we read in this passage that the disciples had gathered in one place. And it was in this house and in this moment in time that the Spirit suddenly showed up. He came unexpectedly, unpredictably, and surprisingly—somewhat like a tornado can, forming without warning and immediately transforming a clear blue sky in an instant. So powerful was this wind-rush that the whole city became aware of it (verses 5-6). It brought such attention to the change taking place that even those who had gathered from their time of Pentecost couldn't help but be aware of what was happening at this house.

This unique location, this house, was invaded from above with a noise that could not be denied. It was as if a nice, sunny day with no breeze in the air immediately turned into a tumultuous experience. It was like a violent, rushing wind blew through and affected all in its path. What's more, this wind came accompanied by tongues of fire. This was no ordinary storm. It had all the elements of a complete transformation.

Now, as we've often seen in California, Colorado, and many areas in the United States and around the globe, when fire is mixed with wind, we have a problem. We have a runaway blaze. We can have fire without wind, or wind without fire, but if wind catches hold of fire, it becomes something different altogether. It becomes that which is nearly impossible to contain and control.

We're told the Spirit came like a violent, rushing wind accompanied by fiery tongues. He came in such fashion that the whole city became instantly aware. This unmistakable presence of God's reality amid God's people transformed both the landscape and the atmosphere as it ushered in the beginning of something entirely brand-new: the church.

Both the anatomy of wind and fire are unmistakable. They are both uncontrollable. Both are transformative. Both are power-generating. Both are cleansing agents. Both are penetrating. Both are unpredictable. The Holy Spirit represents all of these realities when His presence is released and manifested through His people.

THE CHURCH IS LAUNCHED

What I want you to notice, though, is that the onset of the church did not come tied to a building. Neither was it tied to elaborate programming or entertainment. It wasn't tied to super-personalities or spiritual influencers in society at large. And the disciples didn't charm their way into the hearts and minds of a following in order to launch a church. Rather, these disciples had been afraid. They'd been so scared that they were huddled in a room together when Jesus walked through that door in John 20. They hadn't been out promoting their latest book or product. None of those things even existed.

What caught the attention of God's people and even those who were not yet believers was entirely this supernatural invasion of the Holy Spirit. It was all Spirit. It wasn't Spirit plus celebrity spokesperson. Nor was it Spirit plus great food and activities. Neither was it Spirit plus a worship band or a new album of songs. The launch of the church was carried out by the presence of the Spirit.

Unfortunately, today the Holy Spirit has far too often been replaced with sophisticated twenty-first-century formalized Christianity. We often celebrate our facilities more than we celebrate the Spirit. We lift up human personalities more than we lift up the Spirit. We give awe to success and fame more than we do to the Spirit. We have sought to replace Him with entertainment and emotionalism and then wonder why the church isn't on fire.

But why would the church be on fire when we have marginalized the Spirit to our own talents and agendas? Why should the world pay attention to formalized religion when it operates outside of the power of the Spirit?

The people in the culture we read about in Acts 2 couldn't help but notice the Spirit and what He was doing. They couldn't help but turn their heads and acknowledge that something powerful—something different and something new—was going on. It would have been nearly impossible for them to ignore the blaze of the Spirit blowing through, transforming everything it came in contact with. Unlike today. Today, the world can easily ignore the church when it functions in her own power absent the power of the Spirit.

How can we have all of these churches on all of these corners with all of these buildings and all of these programs led by all of these preachers and leaders using all of these mechanisms of communication yet still have all of this mess? There's a dead monkey on the line somewhere, and it's my contention that the dead monkey is the absenteeism of the Holy Spirit. Because when the Holy Spirit shows up, you know it. Just as He did in the book of Acts, God lets you know through a spiritual invasion of this third member of the Trinity. When the supernatural enters the natural, you can't help but notice. While the Holy Spirit is invisible, His presence and influence are quite visible.

No matter how bibliocentric and orthodox preachers are, if there's no power operating in their lives from the Spirit, or in the lives of the listeners in their churches, what is said and taught becomes mere information. Mere information is soon forgotten. Only the Spirit creates the transformation that ignites a life, a family, or an entire church so they can ignite the community or city they're in.

We're living in a time when the Spirit of God has been sidetracked. He's been marginalized. Yes, we hear the Spirit mentioned here or there, but we don't see a rushing wind. We don't see tongues of fire. We don't witness people lit by the presence of God infiltrating the church of God through the manifest presence of the Spirit. The church is not just a spiritual classroom for instruction. It's certainly not a theater for performances or an organization simply for programming. The church is to be the transformational environment for the Spirit of God to affect, infect, and ignite the people of God, resulting in transformed lives that then transfer the values of the kingdom of God to others.

None of us wants to dine in a place that doesn't smell good. Stale air doesn't increase a person's appetite. And none of us wants to eat stale food. Yet somehow we accept stale worship, stale preaching, and stale listening at the majority of our churches today because we don't have the wind and the fire of the Holy Spirit igniting something fresh and new.

We live in a day when the church volunteers to be a mere social club or source of entertainment. That's because we've allowed ourselves to become stale. When there is no sudden wind nor sudden fire of the Holy Spirit lighting the hearts and the spirits of the children of God, the most we can hope for is a community center with a cross on top. If the preacher is the one drawing in the audience or the musicians are the ones filling the pews but people rarely come simply to spend time together in God's presence, the purpose of the church has been corrupted.

The disciples received the power of the Holy Spirit when they were obedient to Jesus' instructions to go and gather in God's presence. They were to wait until the Spirit came to them. Yet most people today don't wait. Rather, they go to church to hear someone speak or to check church attendance off their list. But then they wonder why their lives lack the vibrancy that so often identifies a close follower of Jesus Christ.

That's why prayer was such an important part of the early church. Believers spent time in the presence of God because they knew how much they needed the wind and the fire. They knew they couldn't launch and spread their reach on their own merits. They had to hang out in the Spirit's presence in order to usher in a greater experience of His reality in history. This wasn't a book to read or a topic to study for them. This was something—and Someone—they knew firsthand. They had seen Him work, and they knew if they wanted to accomplish anything at all, it would be because of the power of the Spirit, not because of their own skills, talents, or vision.

The role of the Holy Spirit is to make the truth of God experiential in the life of people. For the unbeliever, it's to make them aware of the reality of sin and then lead them to salvation (John 16:8-11). For believers, it's to transform us into the image of Christ (2 Corinthians 3:17-18). For the life of the church, it's to equip the church so that we are then infiltrating the culture with the presence and power of God.

If and when any of those things aren't happening—people aren't being saved, saints aren't being transformed, and the church isn't making a difference in culture—it's because our relationships with the Holy Spirit have become so dumbed down and dull that He's not free to do His thing in and through us. The Holy Spirit becomes free to flow when we, as the disciples, obey the instructions of Jesus and prioritize the seeking of His presence.

GATHERED TOGETHER AS ONE

Not only were the disciples waiting on the presence of the Spirit as Jesus had instructed them, but they were gathered in one place, as one body. They were together on the same page looking for the same thing. This truth brings in the biblical doctrine of unity. Because the disciples were operating on the same vibe and seeking the same thing while being pointed in the same direction toward the same goal, they received the wind and fire of the Spirit.

The church as we know it today, and we as individuals, will not see the full force of wind and fire on earth until we start taking the biblical doctrine of unity seriously. Satan spends a lot of time disunifying us illegitimately.

Now, there is a legitimate basis for disunity, involving sin and righteousness, or idolatry versus the true God, or even false doctrine and true doctrine (Romans 16:17; 2 Corinthians 6:14; Ephesians 5:11; 1 Timothy 4:1-7; 1 Corinthians 5:1-6). But other than these, there is no legitimate basis for disunity. And yet today our churches and our members are disunified over any number of nonessentials over which we so vehemently find ourselves split—like denominational affiliation or preferences, or more serious disagreements concerning racial issues, politics, or even conspiracy theories—have also kept the Spirit from expressing Himself fully as a violent rushing wind and fire.

One of Satan's oldest tricks is division. He divides believers along illegitimate lines and thus pollutes the atmosphere for any real presence of God to appear. Satan disunifies marriages so that prayers will be hindered (1 Peter 3:7). He disunifies pastors, deacons, and members of churches so that impact in the culture will be held back.

Because God values unity so highly, and He limits His involvement where disunity prevails, it's critical for us as His body to make the intentional pursuit of unity a priority. One of the most important things a church can do is promote Paul's plea in Ephesians 4:1-3:

> I, the prisoner of the Lord, implore you to walk in a manner worthy of the calling with which you have been called, with all humility and gentleness, with patience, showing tolerance for one another in love, being diligent to preserve the unity of the Spirit in the bond of peace.

If and when a church does not preserve spiritual unity, they won't have a significant spiritual presence. If you don't have spiritual presence, you won't experience spiritual power. If you don't have spiritual power, you won't experience transformation, impact, or growth. You'll just have church instead of real change.

I don't know about you, but I don't want to just have church. I don't want to show up day in and day out to entertain people just for the sake of passing the time. I want the Holy Spirit to show up and usher in true change in people's lives—change that then replicates into more change as the wind and the fire of the Spirit spread across our nation and our world.

I believe that during the pandemic shutdown in 2020, God reset our spiritual lives by getting us out of the routine of church attendance and into what matters most. When churches had to close due to the pandemic and people had to search for where and how they were going to get connected with other believers, it was as if the wind and the fire were blowing through our nation in so many new ways. People started listening to preachers they'd never heard before. They began tuning into virtual small groups they never would have attended before. They started searching Scripture for themselves and seeking God's own voice to lead them.

I can tell you personally that our national ministry received testimony after testimony from people who were impacted during this time of upheaval and grew spiritually, for which we are thankful. People who had never even come across us before. But when the normal routine got upended, like when the disciples huddled together in the upper room, people searched for ways to hear from God. And when His presence met them, He transformed them.

Flipping over a few chapters in Acts to chapter 4, we can see this tremendous change that took place in Peter and John as an example. These two men had been so scared that Peter even denied Jesus not long before, and the two of them had also hid out after His crucifixion. These were timid men, not men you would think would go on to boldly proclaim a message that went against the grain of culture. But in Acts 4, we read that is exactly what these men did.

> When they had been released, they went to their own companions and reported all that the chief priests and the elders had said to them. And when they heard this, they lifted their voices to God with one accord and said, "O Lord, it is You who made the heaven and the earth and the sea, and all that is in them, who by the Holy Spirit, through the mouth of our father David Your servant, said,
>
> > 'Why did the Gentiles rage,
> > And the peoples devise futile things?
> > The kings of the earth took their stand,
> > And the rulers were gathered together
> > Against the LORD and against His Christ.'
>
> For truly in this city there were gathered together against Your holy servant Jesus, whom You anointed, both Herod and Pontius Pilate, along with the Gentiles and the peoples of Israel, to do whatever Your hand and Your purpose predestined to occur. And now, Lord, take note of their threats, and grant that Your bond-servants may speak Your word with all confidence, while You extend Your hand to heal, and signs and wonders take place through the name of Your holy servant Jesus" (verses 23-30).

By Acts 4, when the events in this passage took place, the church had already been established. But it was the same principle of unity and the same presence of the Holy Spirit that shook things up wherever the disciples went. Notice in the earlier part of the passage that the disciples did what they did through prayer and unity. It says, "They lifted their voices to God with one accord." When this took place, the Holy Spirit showed up and took over the atmosphere. He lit the place on fire.

Many of our problems today stem from an atmospheric issue. Yes, we have well-conditioned buildings with heating and cooling as we need it, but by and large, our buildings exist devoid of the permeating presence of the Spirit. Because of this, we never get to experience shaking as we should or a supernatural intervention taking place. We don't get to witness the transformational work of God as He blows our minds again and again. We have essentially scheduled and programmed ourselves right out of God's presence.

The Holy Spirit doesn't abide by our programs. He is like the wind. Wind is unpredictable. Wind goes wherever it goes whenever it goes, and it does whatever it does when it does it. And when wind and fire mix, they take over the joint altogether. They'll be jumping over highways to get where they want to go.

That's why we must return to what it means to function as a church where we leave room for the Holy Spirit to move and flow freely. That doesn't mean we fail to plan. We are to have plans, but we're also to submit them to the Holy Spirit so He has the freedom to suddenly set things on fire. We have to leave room again for the Spirit, like the disciples did and the early church members did and all of the great leaders of historical revivals did. Our nation needs a fresh wind and a fresh fire to blow through it. But this will take place only when we become fully committed to prayer, abiding, and unity with one another as we intentionally seek the Spirit.

When was the last time you were shocked by the movement of the Spirit? When was the last time your church was so moved by the Spirit that you were rocked by His power? Our testimonies should never be about just what God did a decade or more ago. God is an ever-present Spirit wanting to move, change, direct, and transform everything in His path. But He does this according to His prescriptive means. We must take seriously Hebrews 10:24-25, which says,

> Let us consider how to stimulate one another to love and good deeds, not forsaking our own assembling together, as is the habit of some, but encouraging one another; and all the more as you see the day drawing near.

DON'T BE A STAND-ALONE CHRISTIAN

Part of who we are as believers in Christ involves how we treat and interact with one another. Kingdom living includes the intentional encouragement and support of others in the context of a healthy relationship. Any Christian not a vital part of a local assembly of believers is, simply put, living in sin. I know that's a harsh thing to say, but I say it only because God says it. We are not to forsake our own gathering together. And while it's true that you don't need to go to church in order to go to heaven, you do need the context of church to encourage others in the faith and let them encourage you.

Also, when you speak or think only about your pathway to heaven, you're considering only yourself. One log in a fireplace will produce only so much heat. Yet when multiple logs are lit together, enough heat is produced to fill a room. We are to love one another, lift up one another, show hospitality to one another, and so much more. It's impossible to do those things alone.

If you choose to be a stand-alone Christian, you are not functioning "in one accord" in the unified body of believers. You will not benefit from them, and they will not benefit from you. What's more, the culture at large won't benefit from the manifest presence and power of the Spirit, who shows up when we gather in unity. God didn't create the church just so its members could sit, soak, and sour. He wants you in a church in order to rub off on somebody else and so that others can rub off on you.

When the Spirit enters an environment of unity, He sets it aflame. When a church is set on fire, it affects everything around it for God's glory and for good. And just as a raging fire can jump a highway, the Spirit can jump from person to person, bringing His transformative work to everyone.

God designed and desires that His people gather in a local church. That's how He set up the strategic advancement of His kingdom on earth. The more logs in the fire, the better. He wants His church aflame with the Holy Spirit so that the transforming work of His presence changes the world.

THE WIND AND FIRE IN YOU

If we return to Acts 2 and read more on the experiences of the disciples after the Spirit reached them, we'll see how God goes about changing the world through His engagement with His followers. We witness His power expressed supernaturally in the disciples' lives.

> They were all filled with the Holy Spirit and began to speak with other tongues, as the Spirit was giving them utterance. Now there were Jews living in Jerusalem, devout men from every nation under heaven. And when this sound occurred, the crowd came together, and were bewildered because each one of them was hearing them speak in his own language. They were amazed and astonished, saying, "Why, are not all these who are speaking Galileans? And how is it that we each hear them in our own language to which we were born? Parthians and Medes and Elamites, and residents of Mesopotamia, Judea and Cappadocia, Pontus and Asia, Phrygia and Pamphylia, Egypt and the districts of Libya around Cyrene, and visitors from Rome, both Jews

and proselytes, Cretans and Arabs—we hear them in our own tongues speaking of the mighty deeds of God." And they all continued in amazement and great perplexity, saying to one another, "What does this mean?" (verses 4-12).

The Holy Spirit gave the disciples the ability to speak human languages they had never learned to speak. The supernatural power took over in such a way that they were able to do what was not natural for them to do on their own. This is how we know it was the Spirit at work and not merely the talents of men.

As a believer, you will also know when the Spirit is working in you, because He will enable you or strengthen you to do what you could never do on your own. It might not be to the extreme of speaking in another language, although it could. But the Spirit will often give people greater confidence, sharper insight, clearer direction, or even a thought that opens doors for them to serve God in ways they never even imagined on their own.

If when I was a small child you had told me I would spend my life speaking in front of thousands of people on a regular basis, I would have questioned you. After all, I had a persistent stuttering problem. But nothing like that matters to God. The Holy Spirit can overcome and overpower any inadequacy we may face in our physical form. And what's more, He will often do that so we'll know that whatever we've accomplished in His name was done by His ability to work His will through us.

Why are we not experiencing more miracles and works of God among us as a body of believers today? Because we have relegated the Holy Spirit to a topic to study once a quarter or a sermon to preach when it fits. We are not full of the Holy Spirit's presence as we should be. And because we are not full, we lack His transformative and miraculous power. Only when we function in His full presence through a committed relationship with Him will we experience His wind and His fire setting things aflame in our hearts and in our lives.

The kingdom impact God wants you to make will, more often than not, take you outside of your natural abilities. It will extend you beyond your natural expressions. It will require boldness where you once were scared. It may include an opportunity for service in an area you never thought you would serve in. The Spirit will blow your mind in your own unique way when you allow Him to infuse you with His wind and His fire.

THE WIND AND FIRE IN US ALL

God doesn't want more programs, more personalities, and more platforms. He wants the Holy Spirit operating in His church in such a way that the culture around us can only turn their heads toward us and say, "Their impact is great."

One look around our culture today and we all know that we desperately need the fullness of the Spirit in each of us individually and in our churches collectively because we face enormous challenges. Our families, communities, and nation have so many complex issues at hand. But we, Christ's followers, are the ones chosen to advance God's kingdom agenda by promoting kingdom solutions to life's chaos in our land. We do this through prioritizing the Spirit's presence so that He can be set free to usher in radical change in a culture that is crumbling before our very eyes.

When baseball players are hitting every pitched ball or quarterbacks are completing every pass, people say things like, "They're in the zone." In other words, they're in the flow where everything is clicking for them and it's all coming together as it should. The Holy Spirit can do the same for you, and He can do the same for me. He can do the same for our families, churches, and ministries. He wants all of us as kingdom followers to live in the spiritual zone. He wants us in His flow. He wants us to keep our tanks so full of Him that He can fuel our thoughts and decisions in order to bring God glory and others good.

Our culture is in decline. Our world is in chaos. Our enemies of the faith are getting bolder than ever before. But we can make a difference when we allow God to fill us with His Spirit so that we're operating in the zone. In His kingdom zone is where real solutions are found. In His kingdom zone, true stability is actualized. And when we're in His kingdom zone, the world will know where we stand. Secularism, socialism, communism, and even capitalism can't mess with God's kingdom and His people when we flow in the power of His Spirit.

God calls this reality being part of His unshakeable kingdom. We read about it in Hebrews 12:28-29: "Therefore, since we receive a kingdom which cannot be shaken, let us show gratitude, by which we may offer to God an acceptable service with reverence and awe; for our God is a consuming fire." You and I belong to something the world cannot mess with anymore. We're involved with something politics can't invade. As Christ's followers, we're part of God's unshakeable kingdom rule. This ought to give us greater courage. It ought to embolden us to live faithful lives under His leading and care. It ought to motivate us to pursue the filling of the Spirit as a regular part of our lives.

In Acts 2, the church looked good and brought God glory because it was burning with the consuming wind and fire of the Holy Spirit. We are to do no less today. People should be seeing what's going on in our lives, homes, churches, and ministries and ask how they can be a part of it. They should want to know how we did what we did. Because when the church and her members are so filled with the Holy Spirit, the world will take notice. Impact will occur. Transformation will sweep over our land and around the world as God's people filled with the wind and fire of His Spirit make His works known to the glory of His name and the advancement of His kingdom on this earth.

THE URBAN ALTERNATIVE

The Urban Alternative (TUA) equips, empowers, and unites Christians to impact individuals, families, churches, and communities through a thoroughly kingdom-agenda worldview. In teaching truth, we seek to transform lives.

The core cause of the problems we face in our personal lives, homes, churches, and societies is a spiritual one. Therefore, the only way to address that core cause is spiritually. We've tried a political, social, economic, and even a religious agenda, and now it's time for a kingdom agenda.

The kingdom agenda can be defined as the visible manifestation of the comprehensive rule of God over every area of life.

The unifying central theme throughout the Bible is the glory of God and the advancement of His kingdom. The conjoining thread from Genesis to Revelation—from beginning to end—is focused on one thing: God's glory through advancing God's kingdom.

When we do not recognize that theme, the Bible becomes for us a series of disconnected stories that are great for inspiration but seem to be unrelated in purpose and direction. Understanding the role of the kingdom in Scripture increases our understanding of the relevancy of this several-thousand-year-old text to our day-to-day living. That's because God's kingdom was not only then; it is now.

The absence of the kingdom's influence in our personal lives, family lives, churches, and communities has led to a deterioration in our world of immense proportions:

- People live segmented, compartmentalized lives because they lack God's kingdom worldview.

- Families disintegrate because they exist for their own satisfaction rather than for the kingdom.

- Churches are limited in the scope of their impact because they fail to comprehend that the goal of the church is not the church itself but the kingdom.

- Communities have nowhere to turn to find real solutions for real people who have real problems because the church has become divided, in-grown, and unable to transform the cultural and political landscape in any relevant way.

By optimizing the solutions of heaven, the kingdom agenda offers us a way to see and live life with a solid hope. When God is no longer the final and authoritative standard under which all else falls, order and hope have left with Him. But the reverse of that is true as well: as long as we have God, we have hope. If God is still in the picture, and as long as His agenda is still on the table, it's not over.

Even if relationships collapse, God will sustain us. Even if finances dwindle, God will keep us. Even if dreams die, God will revive us. As long as God and His rule are still the overarching standard in our lives, families, churches, and communities, there is always hope.

Our world needs the King's agenda. Our churches need the King's agenda. Our families need the King's agenda.

We've put together a three-part plan to direct us to heal the divisions and strive for unity as we move toward the goal of truly being one nation under God. This three-part plan calls us to assemble with others in unity, to address the issues that divide us, and to act together for social impact. Following this plan, we will see individuals, families, churches, and communities transformed as we follow God's kingdom agenda in every area of our lives. You can request this plan by emailing Info@TonyEvans.org or by going online to TonyEvans.org.

In many major cities, drivers can take a loop to the other side of the city when they don't want to head straight through downtown. This loop takes them close enough to the city center so they can see its towering buildings and skyline but not close enough to actually experience it.

This is precisely what we, as a culture, have done with God. We have put Him on the "loop" of our personal, family, church, and community lives. He's close enough to be at hand should we need Him in an emergency but far enough away that He can't be the center of who we are. We want God on the "loop," not the King of the Bible who comes downtown into the very heart of our ways. And as we have seen in our own lives and in the lives of others, leaving God on the "loop" brings about dire consequences.

But when we make God, and His rule, the centerpiece of all we think, do, or say, we experience Him in the way He longs for us to experience Him. He wants us to be kingdom people with kingdom minds set on fulfilling His kingdom's purposes. He wants us to pray, as Jesus did, "Not my will, but Thy will be done" because His is the kingdom, the power, and the glory.

There is only one God, and we are not Him. As King and Creator, God calls the shots. Only when we align ourselves under His comprehensive hand will we access His full power and authority in all spheres of life: personal, familial, ecclesiastical, and governmental.

As we learn how to govern ourselves under God, we then transform the institutions of family, church, and society using a biblically based kingdom worldview.

Under Him, we touch heaven and change earth.

To achieve our goal, we use a variety of strategies, approaches, and resources for reaching and equipping as many people as possible.

BROADCAST MEDIA

Millions of individuals experience *The Alternative with Dr. Tony Evans*, a daily broadcast on nearly 1,400 radio outlets and in more than 130 countries. The broadcast can also be seen on several television networks and is available online at TonyEvans.org. As well, you can listen to or view the daily broadcast by downloading the Tony Evans app for free in the App Store. Over 30,000,000 message downloads/streams occur each year.

LEADERSHIP TRAINING

The Tony Evans Training Center (TETC) facilitates a comprehensive discipleship platform, which provides an educational program that embodies the ministry philosophy of Dr. Tony Evans as expressed through the kingdom agenda. The training courses focus on leadership development and discipleship in the following five tracks:

1. Bible & Theology
2. Personal Growth
3. Family and Relationships
4. Church Health and Leadership Development
5. Society and Community Impact Strategies

The TETC program includes courses for both local and online students. Furthermore, TETC programming includes course work for non-student attendees. Pastors, Christian leaders, and Christian laity— both local and at a distance—can seek out the Kingdom Agenda Certificate for personal, spiritual, and professional development. For more information, visit TonyEvansTraining.org

Kingdom Agenda Pastors (KAP) provides a viable network for like-minded pastors who embrace the kingdom agenda philosophy. Pastors have the opportunity to go deeper with Dr. Tony Evans as they are given greater biblical knowledge, practical applications, and resources to impact individuals, families, churches, and communities. KAP welcomes senior and associate pastors of all churches. KAP also offers an annual Summit held each year in Dallas with intensive seminars, workshops, and resources. For more information, visit KAFellowship.org

Pastors' Wives Ministry, founded by the late Dr. Lois Evans, provides counsel, encouragement, and spiritual resources for pastors' wives as they serve with their husbands in the ministry. A primary focus of the ministry is the KAP Summit, where senior pastors' wives have a safe place to reflect, renew, and relax along with receiving training in personal development, spiritual growth, and care for their emotional and physical well-being. For more information, visit LoisEvans.org.

KINGDOM COMMUNITY IMPACT

The outreach programs of The Urban Alternative seek to provide positive impact on individuals, churches, families, and communities through a variety of ministries. We see these efforts as necessary to our calling as a ministry and essential to the communities we serve. With training on how to initiate and maintain programs to adopt schools, provide homeless services, and partner toward unity and justice with the local police precincts, which creates a connection between the police and our community, we, as a ministry, live out God's kingdom agenda according to our *Kingdom Strategy for Community Transformation*.

The *Kingdom Strategy for Community Transformation* is a three-part plan that equips churches to have a positive impact on their communities for the kingdom of God. It also provides numerous practical suggestions for how this three-part plan can be implemented in your community, and it serves as a blueprint for unifying churches around the common goal of creating a better world for all of us. For more information, visit TonyEvans.org, then click on the link to access the 3-Point Plan. A course for this strategy is also offered online through the Tony Evans Training Center.

Tony Evans Films ushers in positive life change through compelling video-shorts, animation, and feature-length films. We seek to build kingdom disciples through the power of story. We use a variety of platforms for viewer consumption and have 120,000,000+ digital views. We also merge video-shorts and film with relevant Bible study materials to bring people to the saving knowledge of Jesus Christ and to strengthen the body of Christ worldwide. Tony Evans Films released its first feature-length film, *Kingdom Men Rising*, in April 2019 in more than 800 theaters nationwide in partnership with Lifeway Films. The second release, *Journey with Jesus*, is in partnership with RightNow Media and was released in theaters in November 2021.

RESOURCE DEVELOPMENT

By providing a variety of published materials, we are fostering lifelong learning partnerships with the people we serve. Dr. Evans has published more than 125 unique titles based on more than 50 years of preaching—in booklet, book, or Bible study format. He also holds the honor of writing and publishing the first full-Bible commentary and study Bible by an African American, released in 2019. This Bible sits in permanent display as a historic release in the Museum of the Bible in Washington, DC.

For more information and a complimentary copy of Dr. Evans's devotional newsletter, call (800) 800-3222 or write to TUA at P.O. Box 4000, Dallas TX 75208, or visit us online at:

WWW.TONYEVANS.ORG

Who Is the Holy Spirit?

With *The Power of the Holy Spirit's Names Workbook*, Dr. Tony Evans will guide you through a detailed exploration of the Holy Spirit's characteristics, duties, and mission among mankind. You'll dive deeper into some of the titles of the Holy Spirit examined in *The Power of the Holy Spirit's Names* and appreciate how He moves within you to shape your personal relationship with Christ.

Written to be used in tandem with *The Power of the Holy Spirit's Names DVD*, this guide is perfect for individual or group study. As you progress through this workbook, you'll discover uplifting truths and fresh insights about the One described in Scripture as *Wind and Fire, Intercessor,* and *Power.*

Your Questions About the Holy Spirit, Answered

With this DVD companion to *The Power of the Holy Spirit's Names*, you can dive deeper into the incredible revelations the Bible makes about the Holy Spirit's unique role, identity, and work.

Perfect for group or individual study, *The Power of the Holy Spirit's Names DVD* illuminates one of the most central components of the Christian faith. You will grow in your understanding, admiration, and love for the complete Trinity as you examine the essential and personal role that the Holy Spirit plays in your relationship with God.

OTHER BOOKS
BY TONY EVANS

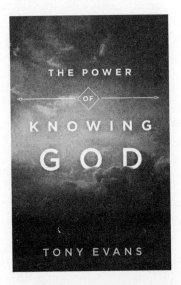

**You go to church, you read the Bible, you participate
in small groups—but do you truly know God?**

God gives every Christian the tools for an active relationship with Him, but many
don't yet experience His presence in their daily lives. Dr. Tony Evans understands
that the only way to deeply know God is to make seeking Him your life's greatest purpose. In *The Power of Knowing God*, he shares how you can prioritize God
over all else—and how doing so will transform you from the inside out.

Your relationship with the Lord can be more than intellectual knowledge, warm
and fuzzy feelings, or dutiful acts of service. As you begin to understand Him personally, you will...

- experience a soul-deep closeness with God
- practice relying on God instead of yourself
- find your identity and purpose in belonging to Him

The Power of Knowing God will remind you that God wants you to be more than
His acquaintance, His student, or His fan, and inspire you to dive headfirst into
the pursuit of a life-changing relationship with your Savior.

Complete your experience with
The Power of Knowing God DVD
The Power of Knowing God Interactive Workbook

"Stop striving and know that I am God." —**Psalm 46:10**

Bestselling author Dr. Tony Evans shows that it's through the names of God that the nature of God is revealed to us. Who is God in His fullness? How has He expressed His riches and righteousness? How can you trust His goodness? As you get to know the names of God and understand their meaning, God's character will become real to you in life-changing ways.

You will explore the depths of God as

- Elohim: The All-Powerful Creator
- Jehovah: The Self-Revealing One
- Adonai: The Owner of All
- Jehovah-Jireh: The Lord Who Provides
- El Shaddai: The Almighty Sufficient One
- El Elion: The Most High Ruler
- Jehovah Nissi: The Lord's Banner of Victory
- Jehovah Shalom: The Lord Our Peace
- Jehovah Mekadesh: The Lord Who Sanctifies
- Jehovah Rophe: The Lord Who Heals
- Jehovah Tsikenu: The Lord My Righteousness
- Jehovah Robi: The Lord My Shepherd
- Immanuel: God With Us

By studying and understanding the characteristics of God as revealed through His names, you will be better equipped to face hardship and victory, loss and provision, and all of the challenges life throws at you.

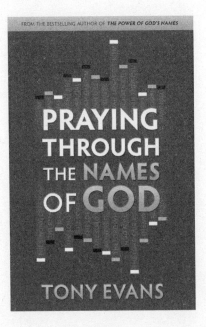

FROM THE BESTSELLING AUTHOR OF *THE POWER OF GOD'S NAMES*

PRAYING
THROUGH
THE NAMES
OF GOD

TONY EVANS

When Life Gets Too Hard to Stand, Kneel

You are called to be a prayer warrior. But which name should you call upon?

God has more than one name—each represents a different aspect of His character. When you know which name to call, you will pray more effectively, and more specifically to your need.

In this book, Dr. Tony Evans provides tools to transform your prayer life as you get to know God in new ways. You will...

- experience God as *Jehovah Jireh*, "the Lord will provide."
- allow God to be *El Simchatch Gili*, "God my exceeding joy."
- make God Your *Jehovah Ori*, "the Lord my light."
- know peace through *Jehovah Shalom*, "the Lord our peace."
- take God as your power source as *Jehovah Uzzi*, "the Lord my strength."
- make wiser decisions by sitting at the feet of *Peleh Yo'etz*, "Wonderful Counselor."

Revitalize your prayer life by connecting your needs with the characteristics of God's names!

THE
POWER OF
JESUS'
NAMES

TONY EVANS

"*Who do you say I am?*"
Matthew 16:15

In his insightful follow-up to his bestselling book *The Power of God's Names*, Dr. Tony Evans introduces you to Jesus in ways you may have never seen Him before. Jesus is anticipated from the very beginning of the Bible and is mentioned many times up until He finally arrives on the scene in Bethlehem—yet never in the Old Testament is He called Jesus. Rather, He has many names that reflect all the different aspects of His character. And there are even more names in the New Testament to explore as well!

Both in-depth Scripture research and Dr. Evans' signature storytelling style make *The Power of Jesus' Names* a fascinating journey—you will get to know Him as

- Immanuel
- King
- Lamb of God
- Great High Priest
- Son of God

As you study the life and character of Jesus, you will enter into a deeper understanding of who He is and what He came to do for—and in—your life today.

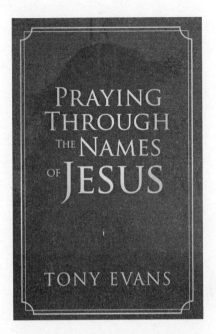

Are You Making the Most of Praying Jesus' Names?

In the Bible, names are significant—an important window into who someone is. The names of Jesus give us rich insight and a deeper understanding of His power, His sacrifice, and His love for us.

In *Praying Through the Names of Jesus*, Dr. Tony Evans serves as your guide as you learn what it means to call on *all* of Jesus' names. As you get to know the significance and power of His many names in Scripture and what they reveal about His character, you will experience an even closer relationship with the Savior.

Through devotions and prayers, you will meet Jesus as Immanuel, Prince of Peace, Lamb of God, Great High Priest, and Son of God. Draw nearer to Jesus and transform your prayer life as you petition His names every day!

Tony EVANS
THE URBAN ALTERNATIVE

Building kingdom disciples.

At The Urban Alternative, our heart is to build kingdom disciples—a vision that starts with the individual and expands to the family, the church and the nation. The nearly 50-year teaching ministry of Tony Evans has allowed us to reach a world in need with:

The Alternative – Our flagship radio program brings hope and comfort to an audience of millions on over 1,400 radio outlets across the country.

tonyevans.org – Our library of teaching resources provides solid Bible teaching through the inspirational books and sermons of Tony Evans.

Tony Evans Training Center – Experience the adventure of God's Word with our online classroom, providing at-your-own-pace courses for your PC or mobile device. Visit tonyevanstraining.org.

Tony Evans app – This popular resource for finding inspiration on-the-go has had over 20,000,000 launches. It's packed with audio and video clips, devotionals, Scripture readings and dozens of other tools.

tonyevans.org

Life is busy,
but Bible study is still possible.

a **portable**
seminary

TONY EVANS
TRAINING CENTER

Explore the kingdom.
Anytime, anywhere.

tonyevanstraining.org

*Subscription model

To learn more about Harvest House books and
to read sample chapters, visit our website:

www.HarvestHousePublishers.com

HARVEST HOUSE PUBLISHERS
EUGENE, OREGON